OUTDOOR LIFE
THE SPORTSMAN'S AUTHORITY SINCE 1898 ®

Classic Stories

EXCITING & TIMELESS TALES
FROM *Outdoor Life's*
GREATEST WRITERS

CREATIVE
PUBLISHING
international

MINNETONKA, MINNESOTA

Creative Publishing international, Inc.
5900 Green Oak Drive
Minnetonka, MN 55343
1-800-328-3895

CREATIVE
PUBLISHING
international

President/CEO: David D. Murphy
Vice President/Editorial: Patricia K. Jacobsen
Vice President/Retail Sales & Marketing: Richard M. Miller

CLASSIC STORIES
Executive Editor, Outdoor Group: Don Oster
Editorial Director: David R. Maas
Editor: Steven Hauge
Managing Editor: Jill Anderson
Technical Advisor: Anne McDonald
Associate Creative Director: Brad Springer
Senior Art Director: David W. Schelitzche
Art Director: Joe Fahey
Photo Researcher: Angela Hartwell
Director, Production Services: Kim Gerber
Production Manager: Helga Thielen
Production Staff: Laura Hokkanen, Kay Swanson

Contributing Photographers: Erwin & Peggy Bauer: p. 183; Stephen W. Maas: p. 164;
Vin T. Sparano: pp. 166, 168; Rick Taylor/*Outdoor Life* magazine: p. 5
Contributing Illustrator: Leon Parson: back cover, pp. 51, 196

Printed on American paper by: R. R. Donnelley & Sons Co.

10 9 8 7 6 5 4 3 2 1

ISBN 0-86573-122-5

Table of Contents

Editor's Note

S everal months ago, we (the editors) contacted our good friend Charlie Elliott, *Outdoor Life* Field Editor since 1950, to write the introduction for this book. After all, in the words of *OL* Editor Emeritus Vin T. Sparano: "No other *OL* editor can match Elliott's tenure or his influence on millions of sportsmen."

Unfortunately, Charlie's health was failing and he was unable to pound out his wonderful words on his manual typewriter. Charlie died a short time later, leaving this world as he put it, "to go sit on a cloud somewhere." While there are certainly other *OL* editors quite capable of handling such a writing assignment, we feel compelled to begin this book in the timeless words of Charlie Elliott:

"Nostalgia is a gem of many facets. Some reflect the bad decisions and mistakes we are unable to erase from our memories. Others shine with beauty or accomplishment that we would like to consider the basis of our true worth.

"Foremost among my happiest memories are the years I have been associated with Outdoor Life — *and with the remarkable fellow writers and editors who dedicated themselves to the creation of a magazine of which we all could be proud."* – From "Men Who Made a Magazine," June/July 1998 *Outdoor Life*

And finally,

"When I go, I want to ask Polly to open the doors of my den and ask my friends to drink all my bourbon."

It is our hope that you enjoy Charlie's 1947 classic, "Wolf Dog," and all of the other great adventures brought to life in this book by *Outdoor Life's* past and present legends.

CHARLES NEWTON ELLIOTT
1906 – 2000

"Adventurer" in the Shark Trade

BY JERRY GIBBS

*What does a 77-year-old
grandmother do for fun?
She tangles with
500-pound sharks, my dear.*

I've always taken sinister delight in the line from Bobby Darin's classic tune "Mack the Knife" about the shark having such pretty teeth, dear.

That the shark keeps them pearly white is good stuff, too, both for the fierce imagery it conjures up and, in a practical sense, for anyone crafting the fish's distinctive dental work into nautical baubles. Which is exactly what Gloria Patience does after she's conquered the beasts with the ivory teeth.

On one such occasion, though, the item most noticeably pearly white was Gloria's blood-drained face.

Anchored in 250 feet of water, fishing down 1,500 feet at the edge of the continental shelf off Exuma, Bahamas, she and her brother were handlining red snappers. They'd been at it successfully for a while, and the cobalt-blue water was rich with bait and scent, and probably a little blood. That's when a middling-size mako shark, about seven feet long, exploded through the silky slick surface and smashed her brother in the neck, sending him to the deck unconscious. Gloria pitched over the side of her Boston Whaler in the continuing pandemonium. The free-jumping shark then disappeared.

"I taught my butt to walk on water in the next two seconds," says Gloria, affectionately known around Exuma as The Shark Lady. "The nearest thing was the boat's bow. Never thought I could climb over it, but I scurried right up like a damned crab." That was some years ago. Her brother still has neck problems. But Gloria's battle-seasoned 13-foot Whaler, *The Nut Cracker*, tooth-scarred and once stolen, is none the worse for the wear in the shark-catching trade. The same goes for Gloria Patience.

She may not fish as often these days, but that's OK. A cadre of international pals—adventurers, artists, scientific types—donate the odd tooth-studded jaw or shark vertebrae, which she pieces-down into necklaces and bracelets. When she does go in pursuit of sharks, Gloria takes a local boat boy with her now to help truss captive, still-living sharks to the boat, but that's her only concession to the years. At 77, she handles a 60-pound grapnel with little more effort than a flower pot, and you would not want to challenge her to a quick bout of arm wrestling.

Four of her nine children, moved in recent years back to Great Exuma Island, constantly worry over her. "They call me up, tell me I shouldn't be chasing sharks, running the damn boat at my age. But I have confidence in my abilities, my dear. If I want to get up and wiggle my butt [she does so], or dance with a drink on my head [she does this also, without spilling a drop], I will."

We are just now at a beach house party on Little Exuma, and Gloria's demonstrations are eye-catching. The explosive yellow of her dress is echoed by the gold necklace and ring she wears against deeply, permanently tanned skin, a mockery of conventional wisdom—as is her style—about the terrors of UV exposure.

Strings of gold beads encircle her ankles and thread between her first two toes, forming faux sandal thongs. She wears no shoes. Never. Not here, not on the mainland nor on the streets of London. "Not for the Queen—even if I had been invited for tea, which I wasn't when I visited there," she says. She fluffs her short silver hair and refocuses those bright, flinty blue eyes that click from mirthful to icicle sharp when the talk slides over to sharks.

For The Shark Lady there is no dark preoccupation with the predators themselves, the infinite brute power of them as nature's ultimate instruments of dissolution. No pathological Captain Quint-like thirst for revenge. No delicious titillative fear of being devoured alive. No thrill for the piston-thump of the 18-inch-barrel marine shotgun (used to quiet the sharks) and its spawn of havoc.

The Shark Lady subdues a still-living shark after hauling it in with her unique fishing outfit. "I do it right, I do it big, I do it with class," is her motto.

Shark collecting to Gloria is the same today as when she was a young girl: utilitarian, a way to make a living, with the added bonus of extreme adventure. And in the early years, possibly as a means of establishing equal footing with male siblings.

"My father showed me—once—how to wade out from the beach with a home-woven line made of silvertops [palmettos] and a brass hook he'd made and baited with a fish head. I learned to tie the line to a buttonwood tree to help me fight the sharks.

"That's how I made my money as a girl. I skinned my sharks and sold the salted skin to the Ocean Leather Company [still going strong in Newark, New Jersey. I used to call myself an adventuress until I looked it up. Honest to God, it means a woman who uses men to get what she wants. I should have used 'adventurer.' I wanted to do everything my father and brothers did."

The Shark Lady did just about that. Straight out of the chute she needed no Equal Rights Amendment for common ground in the true dark ages of male jingoism. Equality Gloria grabbed by the, ahem, ears and made it hers. Over the years came the fellowship, respect and love of men from an odd mixture of worlds that spanned academic, military, art and sports disciplines.

Growing up on her Scots-Irish parents' farm on Hog Cay south of Exuma, she ran the hills like a colt and told the world what she was not about early on. "At age 3 I was kicked out of my first school for beating up a guy and throwing him into a prickly pear tree. They sent me to Sacred Heart [school] in Nassau where I lasted six months and was booted out at age 4½. My father brought me back to Hog Cay where he had hired a tutor I wouldn't listen to. I learned to read and write from a book called the *Mavis Spelling Book.* I cannot be taught, I have to do it myself."

Her approach to sharks is the same.

This is handline stuff. Then again, forget line. She uses 150 feet of braided polyester rope; who knows how strong. To the rope is shackled a six-foot length of chain "leader" and a hook bigger than a big man's foot. A whole grouper head is impaled from the top, the hook point emerging below the jaw. The rig is dropped, the boat moved and anchored so that the line is tight. Sharks up to 10 feet long Gloria simply hauls in. The Shark Lady says she can tell instantly the size of the beasts and you don't doubt it; not from someone who can feel the brush of a red snapper against her baited line 1,500 or 2,000 feet down.

Big things more than 10 feet get the treatment. With the hooked shark going away, Gloria grabs the line and deftly knots to it a short rope attached to a preassembled buoy rig. From the buoy streams an additional 30 to 40 feet of rope tied to a 60-pound grapnel anchor. She heaves the whole works overboard. The rig is now free of the boat. She has yet to hook a shark that has trucked off with her gear. Does she let the creature fight the grapnel and buoy a bit?

"And let some other shark take the fruit of my labor? Oh no, my dear. I go right to it and haul his tail up. It's a neat system."

Alongside *The Nut Cracker's* gunnels, Gloria's methods have come full circle. There was a time when she owned a bang stick that made things simple. "It got their attention; it put a four-inch hole in their heads. But someone stole the thing and now I'm back to tying the suckers up." Which means that, to the amazement of most shark sport fishermen, Gloria snout-ties and tail-ties her 10-foot-and-less catches, heaving them aboard and lashing them down. The bigger fellows are likewise trussed but towed to a nearby beach.

She is fastidious about cleaning her catch. Dragging a shark up the sand, its tail is severed, no blood going back into the water. "In no time he's gone," she says. "It's the quickest way." The back vertebrae and teeth are removed, the body steaked for human consumption or turned into fertilizer. There is nothing wasted.

In 1934, when Gloria was 16, architect and civil engineer James Lewless anchored at Hog Cay on an intended round-the-world cruise. "We fell in love," she says. "I married my first boyfriend. We raised nine children and lived in Nassau where his business was." They were married 27 years, the last 10 of which James, quite considerably her senior, was ill. Gloria turned to other professions to support the family. In her self-taught way, she became a physiotherapist, masseuse and nurse, sometimes working 18-hour days.

She's lived with her second husband, George Patience, for 33 years. Moving back to Exuma in 1970, she transformed the old post office into a cottage, naming it "Tara" ostensibly after the O'Hara homestead in *Gone with The Wind*, but perhaps subliminally for its original reference to the home of ancient Irish kings. "I've always been a romantic," she tells you.

But that truth is intermixed with the gritty realities of making a living. Knowing her childhood waters around Exuma intimately, and finding a ready market with no competition, she began supplying

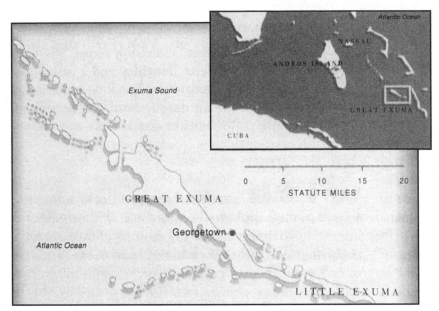

The Shark Lady's home in Great Exuma, Bahamas, is about 300 miles off the Florida coast, 150 miles from Cuba. And the surrounding waters are thick with sharks.

local resorts with fresh fish, handlining 300 pounds of snappers in a morning and simultaneously rekindling her old relationship with sharks. That relationship became all-consuming.

The shark-fighting grandmother's exploits were soon bannered from such widely ranging publications as London's *Tattler* tabloid and *National Geographic* magazine. She has appeared in books, prestigious travel periodicals and on "The American Sportsman" television series. She became pals with *Jaws* author Peter Benchley and a varied cast of visiting sports figures and writers. For R & R she competitively captained a sailing dinghy with a crew of topless women until a rules committee disallowed the team for unfair diversionary tactics.

With sharks, though, Gloria now takes a self-described diplomatic approach. The predators are hunted in channels and in the mouths of creeks back into the mangroves rather than in the open ocean. She refuses to fish in darkness. Her boat is stocked with water, rations and emergency equipment. Twice only has she been forced to overnight aboard the Whaler because of equipment failure. Such inconveniences and inherent risks of the game she accepts almost cavalierly. She has never considered herself in peril, although there was the thing with the tiger sharks once.

Gloria had trussed a 10-foot male tiger to the boat. Some tattered bait remained on the hook, which was thrown back in. "Male tigers are the only shark that lacerate the females with their teeth before they mate, and that's what must have been going on," says Gloria. "We suddenly hooked up again. It was a nine-foot female, her body cut from head to tail. She must have been in a terrible mood from it because she charged the boat and grabbed the gunnel in her jaws. We had to pry her off. The front row of teeth was left in the fiberglass. We got her, though."

The excitement resounds in her voice as she remembers other big fish, and her largest of all: "I had a mean seven-foot lemon shark on when this big mother of a shark came up and swallowed it—all except for the head. She came again, a tiger, 18 feet of her, and took the head and was hooked. When I finally beat her she was too big to tow in and I had to kill her there. She had that lemon shark in her stomach plus a hundred-pound turtle."

Gloria's eyes affect that characteristic flinty-sharp stare as she connects past remembrances with present-day experience. Her enthusiasm continues. "The other day we were fishing a creek for grunts and snappers and there were five lemon sharks there, one of them pretty big. They took some of our fish, our larger fish. I didn't have my shark gear or I would have got them. I still know every worthwhile fishing drop around here, my dear—for dinner fish or for sharks—and I can run right to them without any fancy equipment. I take my bearings and I know exactly where I'm going."

No one would doubt it.

Outdoor Life, July 1994

A Day in Ram Heaven

BY JACK O'CONNOR

Frank Golata using a spotting 'scope to size up two likely-looking rams we had already glassed.

Every hunter of mountain sheep has, I suppose, dreamed of a time when great rams were on every side—so many rams that he was embarrassed and confused by their numbers.

Every sheep hunter has also dreamed that in this ram heaven he'd find his fabulous forty-inch head, the very top trophy in American big-game hunting. In many years of sheep hunting I had dreamed such dreams, but they had never come true. I had hunted sheep from Sonora, Mexico, to the Yukon, and I had never seen a forty-inch head among the many hundreds of big rams I had put the glasses on.

I hoped that when I got to hunt Stone sheep I'd find a forty-incher; but hundreds of expeditions into the northern Rockies, where the Stone sheep dwell, have brought out only about forty rams with curling horns that long. All "outside" sheep hunters are trophy hunters, and the Cassiar district of British Columbia's Stone-sheep country has been hunted for half a century. That a couple of hunters could glass several rams in one day with curls of more than forty inches is so fantastic that it seems incredible.

Nevertheless, that is what happened to Doc DuComb and me one September day on a big mountain off the Prophet River up in the northern part of the province. From a slope on the other side of the river we had seen rams the previous evening, so the next morning we were up early to make the long, tough climb and look them over. I was going to hunt with Frank Golata, the outfitter, and Doc with Mac, the other guide. The frost was still on the grass when we set out and I was chilly even in wool underwear, wool pants, and two wool shirts. I carried a camera, a pair of binoculars, and a rifle. My 20X spotting scope was in Frank's rucksack. Doc and Mac each had powerful binoculars and of course Doc carried his 'scope-sighted .30/06.

We first hiked about two miles to the foot of the mountain. There, before beginning the first stage of our climb, we parted. Frank and I were going to hunt the far side of the mountain, Doc and Mac the near side. Since Frank and I had to go farther, we had to travel faster. Speed in climbing a sheep mountain is only relative, however, and as we toiled up 2,500 feet to timberline we would have looked like a couple of snails to an eagle or a man in a plane.

The mountainside was very steep. First we fought our way through thick black spruce, then through equally thick aspens. Next we struck a belt of high, thick willows, followed by a shale slide so steep that every bit of rock was looking for an excuse to roll a couple of thousand feet. Just before we got over the hump we had to climb a slope carpeted with high slippery grass.

At last, though, we came out on top of the world, in a land of rolling arctic sheep pastures—soft and spongy underfoot, clad in a thick, damp carpet of mosses, lichens, grasses. These pastures were really a series of hilltops that formed a shoulder of a great mountain. They were cut by deep canyons, black with shale, formidable with cliffs; and behind them rose a mighty series of crags black as ink, crisscrossed with the glittering white of everlasting ice that clung to their crevices.

All around us were other upland pastures, tinted in yellow, rose, and umber by the frosts. We looked down on great black canyons, purple timber, and the blue Prophet River meandering through yellow muskeg meadows and dark forest. The great mountain peaks across the river were powdered white with snow, and on their lower slopes patches of golden aspens glowed bright like candles in the night.

We saw sheep almost the instant we put the glasses on the grassy slopes that were still above us—many sheep. Here half a dozen were grazing. There another bunch was lying down. They were more than a mile away, but even at that distance our binoculars showed us that some of them were rams—probably all of them, since in September rams are seldom found with the ewes.

So we set up the spotting 'scope in a little saddle six sheep were feeding. At least three of them were good rams, all of the dark Stone type. Two looked so-so, and one was evidently very young. Above them, lying down on some shale, were three rams—a dark Stone with medium-gray face and neck, and two big rams with faces and necks that were so light they looked almost white, like those of the Fannin variety found in the Yukon. In color pattern the true Fannin is an intergrade between the all-dark Stone and the typical pure-white Dall of Alaska and the Yukon. We were to see other dark-saddled, white-headed Stone sheep that day, but we called them, simply, "Fannins"—and that is how I shall refer to them hereafter.

As we took turns using the spotting 'scope, we picked up other sheep until we had counted twenty-seven in all. That's a lot of sheep, and as far as we could tell all were rams.

The logical way to approach them was to go around and above them, but the wind was wrong, and we were afraid that if we got in line with them, they'd smell us and be off. Frank decided that our best plan was to cross a couple of canyons, then work up another on the far side of the rams, get above them, and come down. To do so we'd first have to lose almost 1,000 feet of our hard-won altitude, but those two Fannin rams looked as if they were worth it. Frank guessed their horns would go close to forty inches, though at that distance it was hard to tell.

Walking rapidly, we started off. We were out of sight of the sheep and had the wind right, when I happened to glance to the left and saw a ewe standing on a ridge about eighty yards away staring at me.

What that lone ewe was doing up there on the mountain with all those rams I do not know. Probably she wasn't all she should be, and anyway her presence was embarrassing to us. If we frightened her and she ran, she might spook all the rams and we'd be out of luck. There was but one chance.

Looking as innocent as possible—as if sheep hunting were the last thing we'd think of—we turned away from the ewe and headed downhill, but she followed along the ridge staring and snorting at us. A little later we could see that she was with four rams that had been hidden from us by a fold in the ground. They were alert, but not very frightened, and they trotted off.

We dropped down into a deep canyon, climbed out, went over another shoulder low enough so the rams could not see us. Now and then we'd stop to get our wind and to put the spotting 'scope on the big fellows. Our two big Fannins were still at their stand, but most of the sheep had worked somewhat higher. Everything was still under control.

By noon we were at the edge of a tremendous canyon and well on the other side of the rams. If our luck held we could work along for another mile, then climb above the rams, size up their heads once more, and work near enough for a shot. Then two things happened which sent my heart right to the bottom of my hobnail boots. First I heard Doc shoot four times on the other side of the mountain, and I was afraid that those two big Fannins would pull out for the cliffs. Next we rounded the bend of the canyon and ran into four rams. We were afraid that they would run over the crest and scare the others.

Actually, one of the rams wasn't a bad one. His horns would probably have gone thirty-eight inches—maybe thirty-nine. He and three smaller rams lay in beds that they had pawed out of the shale across the canyon. They were about 250 yards away and they saw us instantly as we came around the bend, picking our way precariously along our side of that cliffy canyon.

They watched us. We watched them. They grew more and more nervous, and finally they got up and ran in single file along the side of the canyon, down into the bottom, and then finally up the head of one fork and out of sight. We had a break there. If they had crossed the canyon to our side but higher up and run over the ridge, the rams we were stalking would have seen them and would have known that something was amiss.

At last we negotiated our mile along the wall of that canyon. We were about six miles from camp and something like 3,500 feet above it. We had only to climb to the crest of the ridge to our left and, staying under it, work up higher than the rams. Then, after crossing the head of the canyon that separated us, we would be above them.

We had got almost to the top of the ridge when we paused for a moment to get our wind. I happened to put the glasses on the head of the right fork of the canyon we had just left—and there in the saddle, about a mile away, I could see twelve rams. About half of them were lying down. The other half were feeding. Through the binoculars they looked good; and through the spotting 'scope one of them looked colossal. Even at a mile it was easy to see that here was one ram in many hundreds, a fellow with long and massive horns.

"Get a load of that fellow lying down in the middle of the bunch," I told Frank. "If that isn't a forty-inch head I'll never in my life see one!"

Frank took a long, long look through the 'scope. Finally he passed judgment: "I think that will go forty inches myself!"

"O.K.," I said, my aching joints forgotten, "let's take out after him."

To get a shot at the big boy, we would have to climb up a very steep, boulder-strewn canyon, then go over a ridge, up to the head of a second canyon which headed close to the saddle where that big bunch of rams were resting and feeding. In doing this we'd have to turn our backs on the two big Fannins we had been stalking since morning, but the chance was worth taking.

So, instead of getting above the first rams we had put the finger on, we began the long and painful climb over the boulders of that big canyon. The sun was bright and warm. We hadn't had a drink since early morning and we were very thirsty. As we clambered from boulder to boulder we could hear water running through the rocks below us. Our mouths were cotton-dry and the icy tinkle was tantalizing. It was tough going, as some of those boulders were too smooth to hold hobnails.

Gradually, though, we pulled up higher and higher. We found a little old snow, ate it, and thus relieved our thirst. Finally we had only about 100 feet to climb until we could get over the ridge into the next canyon and begin the final stage of the stalk on this fabulous forty-incher.

Then, right over where the two big Fannins were, we heard a fusillade of shots: One-two-three-four-five-six-seven-eight. . . . From the fact that sometimes we could hear the crack of the bullets before we heard the boom of the report we knew that Doc was shooting across the next canyon in our direction. He had got into the big bunch of rams we had planned to stalk before we saw that forty-incher.

My heart sank. It looked as though our day was wasted; all that heart-breaking, leg-straining climbing in vain. Big rams are wary creatures, or they don't live to be big rams, and I was sure that our forty-incher had pulled out by the time the second shot went off, even though he was more than a mile away.

"Oh, nuts! What a break!" I moaned. "We might as well forget that big baby!"

"Don't feel too bad," Frank tried to comfort me. "We're in a good spot, with only a ridge between us and all those rams. Maybe something nice will run over us."

There was nothing for us to do except to sit and see what breaks we got. If some of the rams ran directly away from Doc and tried to put a ridge between them and the muzzle of his rifle, they would come around the point and along the other side of the canyon where we sat. That looked like the best bet at the moment, so we waited …

To back-track for a moment: Earlier in the morning Doc and Mac had seen a good lone ram on the other side of the mountain. Doc didn't get a good shot at it and his four bullets failed to connect. They then decided to hunt up some more rams, so they had climbed high and had innocently drifted over in our direction.

As luck would have it they ended up on the ridge toward which we had originally headed, but they saw nothing there. Since we had last glassed them, all the bunches of rams we had seen early that morning had come together for a slumber party during the middle of the day, when all respectable rams lie down. They had pawed out beds right at the foot of a cliff. Such being the inscrutable ways of fate, Doc and Mac had decided to go right to the top of this very cliff to look out and see what they could see.

Imagine their surprise to hear rocks rolling, and look down upon something like thirty-five rams, all getting out of there in every direction right under their feet! Some went up the canyon, some down the canyon, some crossed to the other side. Forced to make a hasty choice, Doc decided on a big Fannin with a very wide spread and rolled him over in two or three shots. Then he opened up on a dark Stone-type ram with a massive broomed head. The ram was across the canyon, but finally he got him down.

In the meantime I sat across the ridge in the next canyon with a cartridge in the chamber of my lightweight, fancy .270, muttering to myself and full of gloom. In a short time I saw a ram poke his head over the ridge.

"There's a ram," Frank said.

"He's not worth shooting," I growled.

"Maybe some more will come around."

The ram, about five or six years old, stopped just on our side of the ridge and glanced in our direction, but did not notice us because we remained absolutely frozen. Then another ram showed up, a good big Stone with a fine massive head and what I judged to be 38 or 39-inch curls.

"That's a nice ram," Frank whispered.

"He won't go forty inches, though," I said.

"No," Frank agreed. "I don't think he will."

Then a third ram came around. He was a husky Fannin, probably one of the two we had seen that morning. Right at his heels came a fair-to-middling Stone. All looked back over their shoulders at the place where the shots had come from, but they didn't appear very frightened and they had not detected Frank and me.

I laid my rifle over my knees and picked up my binoculars. The Fannin was an excellent ram. He had a good long curl with one perfect point and the other slightly broomed, but I wasn't sure they were long enough to suit me, and I couldn't afford to blow my last chance at a forty-incher.

"Think the big Fannin will go forty?" I whispered.

"Close but not over," was Frank's verdict.

The four rams moved slowly along the other side of the canyon less than 200 yards away. The glasses told me that the big boy had a complete curl and then some; but that doesn't necessarily mean much, for I have seen thin-horn rams, both Stone and Dall, that had more-than-complete curls yet didn't go thirty-eight inches.

Then, as the big Stone and the Fannin happened to be side by side, I noticed that the Fannin was a much larger sheep; and on a sheep with a big head and body, the horns do not look so large as they really are.

Right then and there I decided to take him. He was above me and quartering away. I slipped my left arm into the loop of my sling, shifted my heels a little so I was in as solid a sitting position as I could manage on those rocks, and put the intersection of the cross hairs low behind his right foreleg. As I squeezed the trigger I heard the bullet strike and saw the ram spin around.

"His front leg on the off side is broken high!" reported Frank, who was watching with the glasses.

I worked the bolt and shot again. The ram stayed on his feet, so I fired a third shot. At this the sheep went down—and for keeps.

Slowly, wearily, painfully we crossed the canyon and climbed up to where the ram lay. He was a big fellow, as large as most bighorns, and by far the heaviest thin-horn sheep I have ever seen. As we worked closer and I saw those great horns, I could tell they were larger than they'd seemed from across the canyon.

"Will they go forty?" I asked Frank.

"Golly!" he said. "They'll go more'n that! This is the third forty-incher I have ever seen!" (The two others, by the way, were No. 1 and No. 2 in the record book of North American big game.)

Neither of us had a tape, so definite measurements would have to wait until we got to camp. Those three shots of mine, we found, had all struck low behind the shoulder. They had just missed the heart, without opening up much, but together they had almost torn the left front leg off just where it joined the body. It was one of those things. The Stone I had shot previously had been killed instantly with one shot in the same place. This ram had taken three!

I used the barrel of my rifle to get a rough measurement and I couldn't see how those horns would go less than forty inches, but to keep myself from being disappointed I tried to tell myself I wouldn't be too bitter if they went only thirty-nine and a half.

Frank and I ate a sandwich apiece and washed them down with snow. Then, while I started to skin out the head, he went over the ridge to see what had happened to Doc. He came back in time to help me take the head off, cut out the backstraps and hindquarters. Doc and Mac, he told me, were well to the east and toward the bottom of the canyon skinning out a couple of heads, one of which looked fine through glasses.

Camp was about six miles away—and six tough miles. It was then around 3:30 p.m., so Frank and I didn't even go down to see Doc and Mac. Instead we cut straight across for camp. I had the massive 45-pound head and scalp; Frank toted a load of meat. We had hardly started down the steep side of the canyon when I stepped on a loose stone and fell so hard I bounced.

Loaded down as we were, it was a long, tough pull. When we hit the grassy slope I put the big head on my lap and slid a quarter mile down the mountain, using my heels as brakes.

It was 7 o'clock and just getting dark when I staggered up to the cook tent and cried: "Quick, Johnny—the steel tape!"

We laid the big head on the table there in the candlelight of the cooktent. The tape said forty-two inches. I measured it again and got forty-two and a half! Here was my forty-inch head and then some! The circum-

Those horns, I was convinced, would measure at least forty inches along the curl, though I tried to tell myself I wouldn't be too bitter if they didn't.

ference at base measured sixteen inches, which is good even for a bighorn, and simply terrific for a Stone sheep.

It was an hour later and pitch black when I thought I heard footsteps. I went out of the tent and yelled. Doc answered me. He and Mac had missed the tent in the darkness. He had two fine heads. One had a curl of forty-one inches—almost as long as mine—and a greater spread. His other ram had a massive, broomed head, with about a 37-inch curl that was very close, for all the world like that of a bighorn.

Our luck had been incredible. Here were two fine heads—both rating places far up in the list of record Stone sheep—that were taken out of one bunch on one mountain in a single day.

At that, I couldn't forget the one that got away—that fine old ram I was stalking when Doc started to shoot. He was noticeably larger than my 42-incher, and to be that much larger his curls would have had to measure at least forty-six! Doc and I are happy with those two great heads, but we both wonder now and then what our luck would have been if that greatest sheep had been on our side of the mountain!

Outdoor Life, April 1947

My Most Memorable Deer Hunt

BY ARCHIBALD RUTLEDGE

———————— ❖ ————————

In my long and happy life, I have killed many bucks. My most thrilling deer hunt occurred in December of 1942. At the time, my son Middleton, his wife Flora, and their nine-year-old daughter Elise were spending a month on the plantation with me.

The regal stag almost wedged himself between two pine trees, leaving only his breast exposed.

One morning I took them on a deer hunt, and I decided to drive out to Wambaw Corner, a famous buck place. I put my son on a good stand on the old road facing the drive. I then took Flora and Elise to an inside stand on what we called the Dogwood Hill. There I sat Flora on a pine stump and gave her some instructions.

"Don't try to read; don't smoke; just look straight ahead," I warned her. "There may be a great buck in there, and he may come out ahead of the driver and the hounds."

I then walked down an old road and turned toward a dry pond, in which I took my stand. I had not been there 10 minutes when I heard Flora shoot twice. Then she began to scream.

"Oh my God!" I thought. "Her gun went off, and she shot Elise."

I got to them as fast as I could. When I reached them, Flora was weeping like a baby. She threw her arms about my neck.

"Oh, Dad!" she cried. "The biggest buck in all the world, and I missed him!"

I turned to little Elise.

"Did Mother miss him?" I asked her (an onlooker usually can tell better than the hunter whether a deer has been hit).

"Oh, yes," Elise said casually. "She didn't touch him."

Well, that hunt was over.

"ACTUALLY I HAVE KILLED 299 BUCKS IN MY LIFETIME,"
WRITES AUTHOR RUTLEDGE, WHO IS PICTURED WITH THE ANTLERS OF THE BUCK HE DESCRIBES IN THIS STORY.

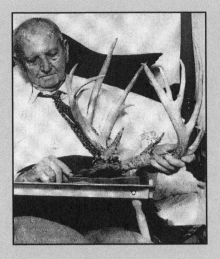

"If 299 bucks seem just too many for one man, I will remind the reader that South Carolina is a good deer state and that some of its zones have the longest season in the U.S. (4½ months). A hunter is allowed five bucks a season, and I have hunted for 78 years.

"As for the use of a shotgun and hounds, they are imperative in many parts of the South, where the swamps are dense and stalking is impossible. I have hunted deer in the mountains of Maryland and Pennsylvania and can readily understand why the rifle is the weapon to use there and why hounds would be out of place. Everything depends on the nature of the terrain. In the lowland South, because of the level nature of the woods, using a rifle would be dangerous."

Before my children left the next day, Flora came to me and said: "Dad, I want to ask just one thing of you. Someday soon go back to that same stump where I was, sit there, and kill that great buck I missed."

It was a large order.

I admired Flora for knowing that an old buck actually has a home he loves in the woods; that although he may be run out, shot at, and even wounded, in a week or 10 days he will return home; and that if run out again he may take the very same course he took before, especially if he has not been wounded.

I waited two weeks before going back to the stump from which Flora had missed the buck. My driver, Prince, took the hounds down the old road to the end of the drive, where he would put them in.

My gun was loaded, and I was cautiously silent. I had a premonition that something would happen. It did.

Between me and the head of the drive was a growth of leafless bushes about 10 feet high. Somewhere in there, as yet unseen, something made a jump. I heard twigs break and the telltale heavy thud of hoofs. The first thing I saw were remarkably tall antlers rising and falling. A huge buck was coming straight for me. By that time I had my gun up. As he came nearer, affording me an exact view, I knew that this must be Flora's buck. I had seen literally thousands of whitetails in the woods, but no buck equal to this one.

I once killed a beautiful 12-pointer that was run to me by a strange hound, which had no business in my hunt that day. Another time, on a rainy day, I shot a buck while he was running through a thicket of scrub oaks that were still carrying their leaves. When I went to him, I noticed at once the extraordinary width of his 10-point rack.

"He is a stranger here," my driver said when he came up. "Heaben is his home."

But Flora's buck was very special, and I thought I had him. But, Brothers, beware the strategy of an old buck if he discovers that a hunter is near. Something unexpected is likely to happen. It did this time.

The regal stag with the spectacular antlers kept coming straight for me. I had my gun on him, but suddenly he stopped. And he could not have planned better for his security. He almost wedged himself between two big yellow pines. He left nothing exposed but his breast, behind which is the brisket, acting as a shield for the heart. When a buck is dressed, a hatchet is needed to cut down through the brisket.

The huge deer was standing about 55 yards in front of me. I knew that if he suddenly drew back and broke away through the thicket, I would have little chance at him. I had great faith in my old 12 gauge Parker double with 32-inch barrels and in the 16 pellets of No. 1 buckshot in the shell in the left-hand barrel. If the buck would come forward on the outside of either pine, exposing one shoulder and flank, I was pretty sure I could put him down. But there remained the possibility of his suddenly drawing back.

The question was simple, but the answer was hard. Should I shoot or not? At 40 yards a shotgun is deadly. The professional hunters of Africa prefer a shotgun loaded with buckshot to a rifle for stopping a charging lion. But at 50 or 55 yards uncertainty begins, partly because of the scattering of the buckshot. A hunter all alone in the woods must sometimes face problems like these, and they are crucial.

I knew that the buck had not seen me, for I had not moved. If a man sits motionless on a stump or a log in the woods, a deer is liable to run over him. A deer's eyesight, except for detecting movement, is not nearly so keen as his nose. But perhaps the buck had located my scent and would draw back, killing my chances. I decided to shoot.

This was to be a standing shot at by far the biggest buck I had ever seen. I confess that for a moment I had a misgiving about shooting so regal an animal. But that foolish idea soon passed, for I have always been a hunter and here was the chance of a lifetime.

My sight was on the buck's breast and my gun was cocked, so I had nothing to do but steady myself and pull the trigger. At the blast of the gun, the mighty buck stood straight up, looking as big as an elk and as tall as a pine. Then he fell heavily backward. But he got up shamblingly and made his way, listing heavily, into a pine thicket so dense that I could not accurately give him the second barrel. I did not think he could go far. How wrong I was!

So many times we do not think, or else think wrongly. For example, I was once on a crossing in the line of an old fence. A few posts were still standing, and one strand of wire was stretched between them. The wire was not two feet above the ground. After a half-hour wait I saw a buck coming my way far off through the pines. He had a noble rack. He was really shoving off, for my driver was whooping it up behind him. If the buck continued on his course, he would cross the fence about 30 yards to my left—a perfect shot.

But when dealing with a wise old buck, a hunter should expect the unexpected. So certain was I that the deer would jump the wire, that I leveled my gun about three feet above it, planning to take him in the air when he made his leap. I had seen him in that part of my plantation several times, so I believed he knew the fence.

As it turned out, that buck knew more about getting past a fence than I did. I had thought he could do it only one way, but there were two.

Just before the buck reached the wire, he dropped to his knees and crawled under the obstruction (tall horns and all!).

Had he sensed that he was in dangerous country and could not afford to display himself by jumping over the wire? I think he never saw me. Because I was so astonished by his maneuver—and perhaps because

I momentarily admired him so much for his strategy—I did not shoot at him. Away he went through the forest, still wild and free.

I think it is a great mistake to suppose that all hunters gluttonously shoot everything they see. A good many hunters prefer to give a wild creature a chance, especially if they have an uncertain shot that may result only in a wounded animal. Personally, I will never shoot at a buck unless I am fairly certain I can kill him.

Here I might remark from my experience that too few deer hunters learn carefully how to judge distance. Is the deer 50 yards away, or 150? At 50 yards a buck can be killed with a good shotgun; at 150 a good rifle in the hands of a skilled hunter will take him.

An amateur hunter once told me he had killed a big buck that had been running through the woods 300 yards away. I judged that he really did not know the meaning of 300 yards.

Every weapon has its own capacity to kill game at a certain distance. A hunter should know this capacity and not expect any unreasonable performance. Also, a hunter should remember that there is a limit to the accuracy of his eyesight.

Now to return to the great buck I had shot and thought I would find. Certainly he had left a heavy blood trail. I saw where several times he had lain down and bled heavily. But a natural misgiving chilled me. Had I, like Flora, let this majestic stag get away?

I decided to return to the two pines to see how many buckshot had saluted them. Then I would know how many my buck had received. As I have said, the shell chambered 16 pellets. When I searched the two pines at the right height I found, rather to my dismay, 12 buckshot holes. Only four could have struck the deer. But from his ponderous fall and from the blood he had left, I felt that one of those four had passed the side of the brisket and had gone through his heart.

Baffled, I thought I had better get my driver Prince and the hounds. Prince is a fine hunter and woodsman, but he is a little deaf. I had a time finding him. When we met an hour later I learned that most of my pack had chased another deer across the river. Prince had with him only Music, a runty, rather bashful little hound, but she had a fine nose.

As we walked up the road together, I told Prince what had happened.

"Music will find him," he said.

The little hound took the blood trail. But before long, somewhat to my chagrin, she began to open and then lit out. From the way she was running, I knew the buck had run a good deal farther than I had thought he would. And following a wounded buck, especially a record one, is always hard on a hunter.

Prince suddenly paused and put his hand on my arm.

"Music," he said, "she quit runnin'."

That should have meant just one thing: she had come on my buck. But it didn't mean that at all, for presently here came Music back, and she was covered with blood. What could that mean? I examined her carefully. The blood was the buck's, not hers. But she was trembling and seemed afraid.

Then, to my relief, we were rejoined by Red Liquor, a big rough raw-bone hound, one of the dogs that had taken a buck across the river. As soon as we put Red Liquor on the blood trail, he went howling away. Music followed, but silently and without enthusiasm. Prince and I followed fast after the dogs. Suddenly we came to an old deep ditch.

As we got to the edge of the ditch, Prince and I saw a great pool of blood, where my buck evidently had collapsed. Music apparently had come on him there and, taking wary note of his huge body and tall horns, prudently decided not to take him on. It has been my experience that most hounds are wisely afraid of a buck with big horns. Music, however, had run down into the ditch, probably inadvertently; hence, all the blood she got on herself.

Meanwhile Red Liquor was clambering westward down the old ditch, which, I knew, ran into an incredibly wild old swamp known as the Elmwood Ricefield. Music decided to join Red Liquor, though delicately. When Prince and I got down in the ditch we picked up the big buck's sprawling tracks. He was running wounded, but I did not think he would go far.

As we hurried down the ditch, Prince paused and again laid his hand on my arm.

"Red Liquor," he said, "he is bayin' now."

As I listened eagerly, I heard Music join in faintly. She, too, was bay-ing, but rather halfheartedly. Either the buck was down or the hounds had brought him to a stand.

The ditch rose to the end of a bank that spanned the desolate ricefield. I walked ahead, my gun ready in case a second shot was needed. It was not. Soon we saw the hounds pulling at something at the foot of a huge cypress. When we came up, there lay my record buck. He was dead.

We were almost in awe. The buck's antlers were beautiful and symmetrical. There were seven points on one side, six on the other. Several of the tines were 14 inches long. His bulk was huge. Later we weighed him on some old scales used for weighing bales of cotton; his weight, before dressing, was 287 pounds. I think it rather rare for a whitetail buck to weigh over 200 pounds. But, as Raymond Ditmars once wrote me after I had reported a nine-foot diamondback to him, "I am not at all surprised. There are giants in nature as in human nature."

Some of the backwoods hunters who had heard of my luck came in to see the big buck. Nearly all of them declared that they had seen him before. Three professed to have shot at him. They were generous in their admiration.

I have killed many other bucks in my lifetime, but none of them ever rivaled that old master. Such was my most memorable deer hunt.

Outdoor Life, July 1971

A Swordfish the Hard Way

BY LARRY LITVINOFF
AS TOLD TO EARL GUSTKEY

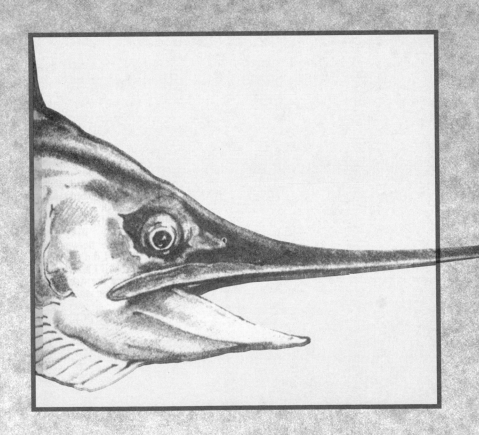

I first saw the swordfish at 7:50 a.m. about 12 miles off the coast. He was 50 yards away, swimming kind of erratically and slowly. He was so big that I was a little afraid of him at first. I figured he was well over 10 feet long.

When I spotted him I was on my way to a point 20 miles off Dana Point, California, where I'd seen a swordfish the previous weekend.

It was July 26, 1980, and my goal was to catch a swordfish while fishing alone in my 17-foot Boston Whaler. This was my sixth serious attempt to find and catch a swordfish alone. I'm a physical therapist, and a weekend fisherman. I own a small boat because I can't afford a big one.

I used to catch bonito as a kid in a skiff at Redondo Beach, California, and pretend I was Ernest Hemingway fighting a marlin. I dreamed then of doing something great in ocean fishing.

All the experienced sportfishing skippers in Newport Beach who'd talked to me about swordfish told me they'd never heard of anyone catching a swordfish alone while fishing from a little boat. I don't think any of them thought I could do it either.

But here I was by myself and staring at one right in front of me.

I put my outboard motor into neutral and prepared to offer a bait to the fish. I told myself to relax, and to do things methodically and correctly, but I could feel myself getting excited. I grabbed the squid I'd bought the night before, and I got a bit angry when I felt it and found it was still half frozen. I held it in the water and kneaded it to break up the ice and make it more supple.

I'd sewn a hook into the squid the night before, so I attached the squid to the leader and then put on my fighting belt. I put the squid over the side and paid out about 60 feet of line.

I put the motor in gear and moved the boat slowly so as to get the squid behind me, watching the fish all the time. The sight of his black dorsal fin and tail on that gray morning was kind of scary. He was still swimming erratically, slowly. I remember thinking at the time that he resembled a person looking for a lost contact lens.

I held the rod in my left hand and steered the boat with my right. I made a slight left turn to put the bait about 10 feet from the fish, and I gave the bait a short, jigging action.

The swordfish turned slowly to the left, away from the squid. So I went around him again and presented the bait once more. This time, from 20 feet away, he turned on it. When he saw it, his fins stiffened. Then he picked up speed and went under.

I jigged the squid twice. The swordfish whacked the squid with his bill. Even with the reel in free spool, I could feel his incredible power traveling all the way up the line to me. Then, two more whacks five seconds apart. Line started going out. I could tell that the squid was in his mouth.

He wasn't swimming fast, just steady. I reached into my duffel bag for my fighting harness, put it on, and clipped it to the reel.

The fish was swimming steadily away. About 45 seconds later I figured it was now or never. I kneeled because I was afraid he might pull me over the side when I set the hook, and I wanted a chance to hit the railing first. At that point I felt a little fear. I I d never caught a swordfish before, and I didn't know what it would be like when I set the hook.

I put my 9/0 reel into gear and struck the fish three times, as hard as I could. The hookup felt solid. What do I do now, I wondered. I thought of stories I'd heard about long battles with swordfish—39 hours, 22 hours, 13 hours. And those were fought by guys on big boats who had help.

I didn't have a deckhand to keep my fighting chair facing the fish, another holding the gaff, or a skipper to run the boat. But I had good gear and I was mentally prepared. Still, I was apprehensive.

In the summer of 1978 I'd caught a 192-pound striped marlin while fishing by myself six miles off the east side of Catalina. But anyone who's caught a swordfish will tell you that if you multiply a hard fight with a big marlin by 10, you'll have a rough idea of how tough a swordfish is.

Catching a swordfish under *any* circumstances is tough. I know guys who've been fishing for swordfish for years and never had a strike. Even if you find one finning, the chances of it going after your squid are well below 10 percent.

I figured the swordfish would run like a train when I struck, but he just kept swimming steadily. He never broke pace.

I had 620 yards of 80-pound-test Dacron line behind 15 feet of monofilament leader and 15 feet of double Dacron line. I tried reeling in. It was easy. *Why is this so easy,* I wondered. Then it hit me: *The swordfish doesn't know he's hooked!* I remembered stones of swordfish that had been hooked for four hours and then suddenly began feeding on mackerel.

He went down and swam around the boat once. Then he came up and jerked his head from side to side three times. He was gorgeous! He seemed to be lit up, a purple-blue fluorescence.

Now he knows he's hooked, I thought. And man, did he take off! He took out 300 yards of line, and it was screaming. The heat on the reel was unreal. He was going so hard the harness was making it hard for me to breathe.

That was 30 minutes after I'd hooked him. With one hand I turned on my radio transmitter and said, "This is the boat 'Lundy Tours.' Are any boats in the area?" No answer. Then I worried that there was no one within 20 miles. I called every 10 minutes for a while. Finally I got a response from a boat called "Lovely Doll."

"What can I do for you?" a man asked.

I said, "My name's Larry. I'm on a seventeen-foot boat by myself, and I'm hooked up with a swordfish. "

"Are you sure it's a swordfish?" the guy asked.

"That's an affirmative," I said.

"Are you sure it's not a shark?"

"That's an affirmative."

"OK, we'll come find you. I've got a big boat and a fighting chair. You can get in my boat."

"No, I don't want to change boats. I want to do it in my boat. I just want to keep in touch with someone, that's all."

Pretty soon, the news was all over the ocean. Many people were talking about it on the radio. I relaxed for the first time and thought, *Hey, it's me, out here alone with a big fish, a big ocean, and my little boat. Am I dreaming this?* What a great feeling! All those people on the radio were pulling for me.

The next 2½ hours were a tug-of-war. The reel's star drag got so hot I couldn't touch it. A couple of times the fish headed toward the boat, and I had to reel in fast. Or he'd be north of me and suddenly head south and turn the boat around 180'. That happened five times. I'd shut the motor off, but during the long fight I turned it on twice and let it run so as to charge the battery.

I changed my position, alternating between my fighting chair in the bow and the bench at the steering wheel. I found that when I was in the chair the boat would move in the direction the swordfish was going. I wanted him pulling the boat sideways so that he'd tire.

It was difficult to maneuver between the chair and the bench. When I did it I'd put the reel in neutral. I felt that if I left the reel in gear there was a chance the fish might yank me over the boat's railing and into the sea.

After the 2½ hours had gone by the fish cut loose with a couple of really hard surges. At that point, I was feeling great fatigue in my hands, forearms, shoulders, and back.

Now came my worst moments. The fish was smoking, and I needed to get into the fighting chair. I jammed the rod butt into the chair's gimbal (a metal cup the rod butt fits into), and the gimbal fell off. The screw holding it to the chair had come out and had fallen through the decking. I pulled up the hatch cover and could see the screw but couldn't reach it. By rocking the boat, I made the screw roll to where I could grab it.

I decided there was no way I could catch that swordfish without repairing the chair. For all I knew then I'd be fighting the fish for 18 hours. So I got a screwdriver from the dashboard and fixed the gimbal with one hand.

My confidence was pretty high, so when I got into the chair I decided to get aggressive. It was close to 11 a.m. I knew that in another hour the wind would start kicking up the sea. I got competitive and went one-on-one with that fish.

The fish had about 300 yards of line out when I started pumping. For half an hour I slowly gained line. The fish got close, and the double line came out of the water. I was excited though I half expected the fish to rip off 400 or 500 yards of line any minute.

Now I was at a critical point. I must gaff the fish. When I had the double line around the spool four times, I gave one last heave on the rod and reached out and grabbed the leader. I saw the fish for the first time since hours earlier, when he'd shaken his bill near the boat.

He looked like a huge black shadow under the water. He was hooked outside his jaw, which is typical of a swordfish hookup. The leader ran down his left side and was wrapped once around his tail. He wasn't dead, but he was spent. At least he looked spent. But I was cautious because I'd heard stories of swordfish going crazy at the gaff, attacking boats or filleting themselves on a gaff.

But he never even flinched when I hit him in the shoulder with a flying gaff. I got a second gaff in his tail, pulled him in close, and got a line around his tail. Then I grabbed him by the bill and whacked his head three times with an ax handle. Then I ran a line through his gill and tied him to the boat.

It was all over. The fight had lasted three hours and 55 minutes. I sat for five minutes and looked at him, wondering if I'd done something no one had ever done. I tried to pull him into the boat but couldn't even lift his head out of the water.

I got on the radio to the "Lovely Doll" again.

" 'Lovely Doll' this is 'Lundy Tours,' I said. "I want you to know I just gaffed a swordfish by myself."

Then I poured myself a rum and Coke and started worrying about sharks.

I headed for Newport Beach to weigh the fish at the Balboa Angling Club. The boat was listing because the fish's weight was pulling down one side. I ran into a sportfisher called "Bess Bet." The three guys on board helped me untie the fish and lift him onto my bow, where we tied him again.

At that point, when I knew the fish was out of shark danger, fatigue hit me hard. My legs went rubbery. I must have talked 20 minutes nonstop to those guys. I borrowed their swordfish flag and ran it up one of my outriggers.

I can't describe the feeling I had, coming into Newport harbor with that fish draped over my bow. It was the first swordfish of the season. People stood on docks and beaches and cheered me. Boat horns blew. I stopped first at Bisbee's tackle shop dock and the people there gave me a bottle of champagne.

There were a lot of people waiting for me at the Balboa Angling Club too. They cheered when I was photographed with the swordfish. He measured 11 feet 6 inches and weighed 336 pounds.

Outdoor Life, October 1981

Landing the Record Broadbill

by Zane Grey

Our big-game fishing editor, William Barber Haynes, in sending us the accompanying photograph and description of Zane Grey's big broadbill swordfish catch at Catalina island, Calif., last July, says: "Zane Grey, noted novelist and sportsman, today holds the world's record for a broadbill catch made with rod and reel. His fish taken recently in Catalina waters weighed 582 pounds, and it took Mr. Grey five hours and thirty minutes to conquer it in what he calls an 'old-fashioned' fight. Mr. Grey holds that there are old-fashioned ways and new methods of doing things, even fishing, and that when it comes to thrill and sportsmanship he favors 'the good old way'."

—The Editor (1926)

For ten years I have been trying to catch a record broadbill swordfish— *Xiphias gladius*—the broad-sworded gladiator of the seven seas. During eight of these long, hard summers my brother R.C. has tried it with me.

During this period I have caught twelve broadbill, and my brother has taken six. Although we have had many hard battles with great swordfish, the longest of which endured eleven and one-half hours, we never have brought to gaff a world's record until this season, when after a tremendous "old-fashioned" battle on the heaviest of tackle I captured a 582-pound fish.

I say "old-fashioned" because the method in vogue here at Catalina during the past few years is a modern one, and like many other modern things in this day and age, is open to question.

Fishermen all over the world hear and read about great swordfish being taken at Catalina, one new record about every year or so. It is very thrilling to read, and no doubt most fishermen wonder how a 400 and 500-pound swordfish can be caught in thirty and forty minutes on rod and reel. But nothing is ever said about the airplane wire leader. This is 15 or 18 feet of wire that holds the hook and is attached to the line. We used to use a piano wire, a very stiff and hard wire, while the airplane wire is thin and pliable, like a cord, and very strong. It loops like a lasso.

Well, the modern method of angling for broadbill is to use this airplane leader, and when the angler gets a strike to slack off a lot of line and let the swordfish get tangled up in it. Sometimes the fish is choked or strangled, and often he is cut to pieces. In any case he is lassoed and hog-tied by this infernal wire. As a result he is quickly pulled in, either dead or unable to fight.

This airplane leader is the deadliest and most unsportsmanlike thing used in this manner that I have ever encountered in fishing. It is also extremely dangerous to the angler. It could very easily loop around his gaff and cut his head off. It would actually do that! And the loss of his fingers is a very great risk.

I did not catch my world's record in this manner. I struck him on a tight line with all the strength I could command and fought him until I killed him. It took five hours and thirty minutes of continuous battling.

If I had not been in splendid physical condition from my hard fishing in New Zealand I never could have whipped the broadbill at all. Nevertheless, I had about all I wanted. My arms and back were badly strained, and my left leg black and blue from constant contact with the arm of the swivel chair. The weight of the fish kept forcing the chair around, and I had to use my legs to get it back straight.

He was not a spectacular fighter. He did not leap or break water. He just fought every way, slow, heavy, with fast runs and deep soundings.

Without the Coxe reel and the Swastika 39 line I never could have conquered this broadbill in any time.

He was the most perfect specimen we ever saw. More than 13 feet in length, 5 feet in girth, with enormous fins and huge, round, curved body, heavy clear to his tail. Without a parasite or a blemish, he was indeed a magnificent specimen of the "King of the Sea."

Outdoor Life, October 1926

The Day Alfandre Fought Geronimo

BY FRANK T. MOSS

Harry was whipping the 14-foot sharpie like a jockey as the giant tuna took them through the fleet with spray flying.

I n the salty village of Montauk, on the eastern tip of Long Island, New York, they still call Harry Alfandre the unluckiest fisherman who ever lived.

Harry was a lean, angular man who had the nose of a beagle for fish, especially tuna. During his days at Montauk, he stirred up storms of excitement and comment by big-city rod and gun columnists.

It was Harry who discovered the famous "Rosie's Ledge" giant-tuna grounds and instigated what amounted to a revolution among East Coast big-game fishermen. Yet Alfandre himself never managed to land one of the great, finned furies that became synonymous with his name. But he tried. Oh, how he tried.

Two weeks before Labor Day in the summer of 1949, Einar Handrup, owner of the commercial fishing dragger Marion H., came into Montauk with a very large bluefin tuna. He had harpooned it somewhere east of Fisher's Island. Harry Alfandre saw the fish, talked with Handrup, and lost a night's sleep mulling over what he'd learned.

The next day Harry took Capt. Clancy Pitts, a local charter skipper, and the crew of the Rosie, his own small fishing cruiser, and shoved off across Block Island Sound for Fisher's Island. With Harry's 15-year-old son Ronald and nephews Howard Alfandre and Sandy Hacker, they were five. After several hours of scouting, they'd found no tuna. A lobsterman they met told them where tuna had been sighted the day before.

When they reached the spot, a couple of miles south of Watch Hill, Rhode Island, huge tuna were breaking all over the place. Four draggers were dashing about, trying to harpoon the fish. One finally got an iron into a tuna. Harry watched and got an idea.

The next day they returned to the spot off Watch Hill, trolling squid and mackerel baits among the rioting tuna. They hooked two large ones, which they promptly lost to broken lines. That evening, back at the Montauk Yacht Club, Alfandre told some of the local guides what he'd seen. They said he was off his rocker because "Tuna don't grow that big in these waters."

The third day Harry lost another fish. When they got home, tired and disgusted, they found Capt. Don Gross of the charter boat Capt. Don preparing to sail the following morning for the big ones. Don Gross knew how to handle big bluefins, and his client was none other than the then Mrs. Dan Topping, wife of the co-owner of the New York Yankees and no mean fisherwoman.

History records that Mrs. Topping caught more dead weight of tuna in the next four days than the entire fleet of the U.S. Atlantic Tuna Tournament, which happened to be fishing at the same time at the Mud Hole of Hudson Canyon, off New York harbor. The fuss the press kicked up over Harry's discovery of the fabulous new tuna grounds and Mrs. Topping's eye-popping catches resounded from Maine to

Florida. In a lyric column in the New York Journal-American, the late Jack Brawley dubbed the spot off Watch Hill "Rosie's Ledge," after Alfandre and his little white boat Rosie. The name stuck.

Local guides quickly quit scoffing and joined the rush to harvest the big fish. Frank Tuma Jr., skipper of the Gannet, brought in seven big ones. Don Gross racked up an even dozen, including the season's largest, a 779-pounder caught by New York sportsman Robert Manger. Captains Ralph Pitts, Bob Tuma, Carl Darenburg, and George Verity, spark plugs of the Montauk charter fleet, helped account for the 25 giant tuna that were weighed in at the Montauk Yacht Club.

Among the tuna at Rosie's Ledge was one monster folks started calling Geronimo. He showed himself occasionally in chum slicks, always far back from the baited hooks. When he joined other tuna in their spectacular surface-feeding, his mighty tail swept like the black scythe of Father Time among the sickle-blade tails of lesser fish. Men guessed his weight at between half and three quarters of a ton.

Harry Alfandre saw and coveted Geronimo. He lay awake nights thinking of ways to hook the elusive monster. But luck was not with him. When summer was over, the Rosie's score was high on broken lines and fractured rods but still zero on big tuna in the boat. Nevertheless, Harry was already planning for the next season, nursing the germ of a radical and exciting idea.

As the summer of 1950 began, Russ MacGrotty inflamed tuna-season hopes by his early capture of a 409-pounder at Rosie's Ledge. Tuna guides and anglers flocked to Montauk as the fishing picked up. Chissie Farrington broke her own women's world record with a 674-pounder caught on 24-thread tackle.

Then came the electrifying news that old Geronimo, grown even bigger and more wary, was back. This was all Harry Alfandre needed to hear. He had refurbished the Rosie, bought new tackle, and hired quiet, capable Oscar Rodge as skipper. An old-time Montauker, Oscar had an unshakable Scandinavian faith that anything the crew of the Rosie set out to do, it could accomplish.

Oscar had built Harry a 14-foot rowing sharpie and placed in its bow a cut-down fishing chair. Alfandre's new plan was to try to catch giant tuna from the sharpie in the manner of the old-time whalers' Nantucket sleighride, fighting the fish from the chair in the sharpie with rod and reel. People scoffed, but not to his face. Folk had learned that Harry's vinegary tongue could marinate those who tried to twit him. Even his wife Rose, for whom the Rosie was named, said nothing.

Then came the fateful day, Sunday, August 13. The weather was ideal for tuna fishing and a long file of sport-fishing boats roared from Montauk toward Rosie's Ledge, 12 miles across the Sound. The Rosie, towing her sharpie, wallowed in the wakes of more powerful and dashing cruisers. Most of the fleet was already anchored and chumming when the small, white boat arrived and planted her mud hook.

The art of chumming consists of doling overboard a thin soup of ground menhaden mixed with sea water and laced with chunks of cut whiting or menhaden. It's a messy and often smelly process, but it does attract big tuna. Alfandre placed the heavy fiberglass rod with its 14.0 reel filled with 54-thread line in one of the cockpit rod holders. He hooked on a 15-foot cable leader, baited the 13.0 Sobey hook with a whole, fresh whiting, and drifted the bait deep behind the boat, tending the line by hand. The others, Ronnie, Howard, and Oscar, cut bait or dipped chum.

Suddenly a motor coughed to life down the long line of anchored boats and one of the chumming vessels slipped its buoyed anchor cable, speeding off in circles, fighting a freshly hooked giant tuna.

"Watch for fish in our chum slick," Alfandre warned his crew, knowing that where one big tuna strikes, many more may be feeding.

Then he felt an incredibly heavy weight on his fishing line. He had put the bait down 60 feet under the surface, hoping for a large fish. He stripped a fathom of the fishing line from the rod and reel, dumping the slack into the water so the fish would have loose line to swallow the bait. When the line came tight again he yanked on it as hard as he could with both hands to set the big hook.

"I have one on!" he yelled as he grabbed up the big rod.

They managed to get him aboard the sharpie and into the chair without upsetting the smaller boat. Oscar tumbled in after him, releasing the line that held the sharpie to the Rosie's side. Grabbing up a steering oar, Oscar dug water to swing the small boat's bow after the fish as Harry jammed his calloused thumb down the star-drag wheel to increase the tension.

The rod bucked and cracked. Alfandre shouted. Line whistled out through the guides. Oscar paddled frantically, cursing around his cud of cut plug. The boat started to skim over the water, towed by the hooked fish. Some distance ahead the tuna boiled at the surface. Harry and Oscar caught a glimpse of a great, familiar, scythe tail.

"Suffering catfish, we've hooked Geronimo!" Alfandre shouted.

The sharpie raced through the anchored fleet, spray flying. Harry hung onto the rod with one hand, flailing his fishing cap from side to side in his excitement, like a jockey urging on a reluctant bangtail.

"Outa our way!" he bellowed at the startled occupants of Gene Goble's resplendent Fishangri-La. The tuna took them whizzing under the larger boat's bow.

The sharpie splattered through the gathered boats like an outboard racer that had bucked off its driver. Motors roared into life as skippers suddenly decided to abandon anchor lines rather than risk a ramming from the seemingly jet-propelled skiff and its two wild-eyed occupants.

"Can't you steer this fish outa the fleet?" Alfandre shouted over his shoulder at the drenched, blaspheming Oscar.

Somehow, Oscar managed to shoehorn the sharpie through the mob of boats without scraping paint or chafing the fish line on an anchor warp. Finally, they were clear of the fleet and out in open water. Oscar heaved a sigh of relief, but Harry saw fresh danger.

"Turn the fish back inshore!" he howled at Oscar. "He's taking out to sea at better than ten knots!"

By cramping the boat hard to one side of the tuna's wake, Oscar found he could steer Geronimo back in the general direction of Rosie's Ledge and the chumming fleet.

"Don't let him drag us back into those boats!" Harry screamed.

"Wish you'd make up your mind," Oscar grumbled, wiping tobacco juice and salt spray from his chin.

Meanwhile, the Rosie and another fishing cruiser, the Barracuda, skipped by young Bobby Darenburg of Montauk, were hovering, near, anxious to render aid, but afraid to come too close. The fight between the tuna and the two men in the sharpie settled down to a gut-wrenching slugging match that circled, stopped, started, and zigzagged just outside the fleet.

Once Geronimo sounded and lay doggo, gathering strength. "Gotta get him moving," Harry muttered, yanking strongly at the fish with the heavy rod.

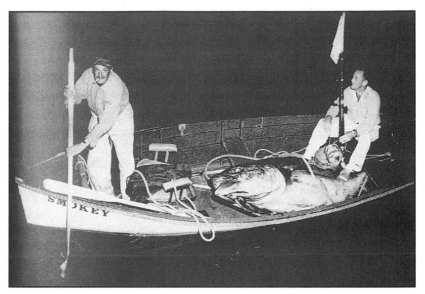
Harry Alfandre paddles sharpie used to fight big bluefins. The angler with foot on conquered fish is A.M. Whisnant.

His problem was a special one. A well-handled power boat can chase and hound a hooked giant tuna into making run after run, burning up its supply of body oxygen faster than this vital element can be replaced by water flowing over the gills. Eventually, the fish can be driven to the point of complete collapse. This is the secret of those startlingly swift victories over huge tuna that mystify so many landlubbers. But Harry and Oscar had no motor with which to chase Geronimo.

All Harry could do was to goad the fish into making oxygen-burning runs by banging at him with the rod under heavy line pressure, then quickly releasing the drag pressure to fool the fish into thinking it was free.

It was back-breaking work. Blisters broke on Harry's hands. He and Oscar were soaked with sweat and salt water. They were dying for a drink. The sharpie needed bailing. At odd moments Oscar flung out a scoop or two of water, but most of the time he had to concentrate on steering and shifting his weight to prevent a capsize.

At last the fish showed signs of weakening. Alfandre increased drag pressure and began to muscle in the last 50 yards of line. He had literally to haul the boat up behind and finally on top of the tiring tuna as it cruised slowly along, a few feet under the surface. Oscar tried paddling, but it didn't help much. The outermost 15 feet of the line was spliced double as gamefish rules allow. When Harry got two turns of this double line on the reel spool he clamped down on the drag pressure to the maximum. The Rosie and the Barracuda cautiously came closer.

Then they saw how big the fish was. "His tail's under the stern of the sharpie," Oscar called out.

"His head's two feet beyond the bow," Alfandre marveled. "He's longer than the sharpie!"

Slowly the fish rose to the surface. Harry winched in the last of the double line until the stainless steel snap-swivel connecting the line to the cable leader touched the rod tip. Dropping the rod, he grabbed the leader and hauled the skiff toward the wallowing fish. Oscar shoved the flying gaff at him. Holding the leader with one hand, Harry made a powerful swipe and drove the hook of the flying gaff into Geronimo's jaw.

He separated the stout ash gaff handle from the detachable hook and hauled tight the half-inch manila rope that was spliced to the gaff hook. The Barracuda had backed close to them and Oscar threw the free end of the gaff rope to Bobby Darenburg, who hauled in the slack and took two quick turns around one of the boat's after bitts.

"He's ours!" Harry croaked triumphantly, picking up the rod to get it from underfoot.

Then Geronimo came to life, showering the two boats and the people in them with sheets of spray from his great, slashing tail. Down he plunged, snapping the gaff rope like string. Bobby Darenburg stood in the stern of his boat, too stunned even to pick up the broken end of the gaff line that hung over the transom.

"He'll dump us over!" screamed Alfandre, staggering under the weight of the fish on his rod.

Oscar scrambled just in time to prevent a capsize as Harry got the reel drag released so the fish could take out line. When they had themselves and the sharpie under control, they were back where they were before the gaffing, but minus the gaff and with the boat half full of water.

"What'll we do now?" asked Oscar.

"Bail out the water, then tire him out and gaff him again," said Alfandre. "What else is there to do?"

Ronnie and Harry
Alfandre with big
tuna Ronnie boated.

Wounded by the swallowed hook and the gaff in his jaw, Geronimo couldn't last forever. Harry goaded him into a couple of runs, but the old steam was not there. Finally the fish was back cruising slowly under the surface, setting its fins against the pull of the line. Harry could gain no more line. They had reached a stalemate. The splice of the near end of the double line was still two feet under water.

Geronimo's blood stained the water. Harry rested, panting, his arms aching. If he could just get in the last couple of fathoms of single line and put two turns of double line on the reel, he would be able to apply enough pressure to raise the huge fish to the surface. Both the Rosie and the Barracuda were standing by to pass them a fresh gaff. He tried once more to raise the fish a bit and failed. Black spots danced in the backs of his eyeballs with each pounding pulse. He had been fast to the tuna for more than three hours, and he didn't know how much longer he could keep up the pressure.

The end came with a shocking suddenness. The hot sun, burning down on the drying linen line just beyond the rod's tip, caused the fibers to lose some of their wet-test strength. Harry took a deep breath and tried to lift the fish, applying a few extra pounds of pressure. There was a sharp snap as the line parted. Harry lurched backward out of the fishing chair. Oscar lunged to catch him.

When they regained their feet they could see the broken end of the white fishing line snaking slowly into the depths as Geronimo's mighty, dying bulk sank away from them.

Numbly they let Ronnie and Howard help them back into the Rosie's cockpit. No one spoke.

The Rosie continued to fish for big tuna at Rosie's Ledge and Harry was sometimes in the sharpie, but there was always someone else behind the big rod. Alfandre's zest for rod-handling was slow to return.

Stan Smith of the New York News hooked a 10-foot shark fishing from the sharpie with Harry at the steering oar. Asked if he had fun, Stan replied, "Fun? It was the second closest thing to suicide."

Guessing at Geronimo's size, good tuna men estimated his length at 14 to 16 feet. He certainly was longer than the 14-foot sharpie. For fish caught with rod and reel, the present world-record bluefin is a Nova Scotia 977-pounder. It measured not quite 10 feet long. A 1,200-pounder brought into Block Island in 1956 by a swordfisherman was short of 12 feet. Using these measurements as rough guides, it's safe to say Geronimo probably weighed 1,600 to 2,000 pounds.

It is fitting to note, in closing, that 16-year old Ronnie vindicated his father's faith in sharpie-fishing for big tuna just three weeks after Harry's debacle. Ronnie took a 676-pound bluefin from the tiny boat in the fast time of 30 minutes flat. When the Rosie returned to Montauk that afternoon with Ronnie's big fish, every boat in the harbor blew its whistle or fog horn. Rex, the dockmaster, fired salutes from the little brass cannon at the Yacht Club.

That night, at the Yacht Club Crew's Bar, a beaming Harry was buying drinks for all hands, satisfied to see his son redeem family honor.

Outdoor Life, April 1964

It always happens when you are least prepared. Traveling through the Alaskan wilderness, you suddenly come face to face with one of the most dangerous animals on the North American continent. What you do in the next few seconds could save or lose your life during that…

Moment of Terror BY MICHAEL A. GANGER

I have had a fair amount of experience with bears, but I cannot recite gospel truth regarding the way to act and defend yourself when a confrontation with a bear is imminent.

You wouldn't believe me, anyway, if I said, "Now, this is just what you should do. Do it and you'll be all right." I wish I did know a foolproof way for an unarmed man to deal with a bear attack, because I'd make a fortune. As it is, I'm content to just not sound like a fool.

I can only provide you with information. I will describe two attacks and give you the benefit of as much experience as I can, but ultimately it will be you who writes the last paragraph of this story. When the show-down comes, only you can determine your fate—I can only provide some guidelines. Whether you triumph and join one of the most select of wilderness groups—those who, unarmed, have faced an attacking grizzly bear and lived to tell of it—or whether you perish, bleeding and mauled along some lonely river in the middle of the wilderness, is decided by just you and that bear.

Hunting grizzly bears is a dangerous business and a tough way to make a buck. Guides and bear hunters are frequently charged. Caribou and moose hunters often have problems while dressing or packing out a kill. Prospectors and miners have their hands full in dealing with bears. Bears walk unhesitatingly right into camps, tearing open tents and eyeballing the inhabitants. I don't mean to imply that Alaska is over-run with bears, but there is a healthy number of them.

Most bear attacks turn out to be a bad move for the bear, because few Alaskans venture out into the wilderness without a firearm. In many towns and villages the wilderness begins about 100 yards outside the town limits. Yet even though men and women are armed and "bear-wise," there are maulings and killings. Sometimes the grizzly just plain gets the jump on them.

When enraged, the grizzly is a formidable opponent. Many men have been cut down while blazing away, fighting to the end. Their rifle did not even the odds enough. But I feel there is a reason that explains, a little more realistically, why armed men are killed. Being aware of this reason is of paramount importance to understanding a bear attack.

When a bear is right on you and coming hard, it's a terrifying experience. It's nothing as simple as blind fear—it's plain paralyzing terror. And I mean *paralyzing* terror. A grown man, for example, should be able to outfight and kill nearly any dog. He may get bitten and torn, but he can shield his throat, get a grip on the dog, throw it on its back and beat it to death. So why is a dog effective as a guardian? Because a snarling, attacking dog is terrifying. The person being attacked doesn't even attempt to fight back, even though the animal is much smaller. Haven't we all seen a grown man backing away from a growling, snapping Schnauzer, asking "Does it bite?"

However, when you're dealing with a bear, the terrorizing effect is multiplied tremendously. Whereas men can become accustomed to handling dogs, very few become accustomed to handling a grizzly. You may hunt bears and live with them around you, but it still won't prepare you for an attack by a determined bear. I believe the shock is so great it causes men to hesitate a critical moment before dealing with the attack, or causes them to attempt something foolish such as turning and running rather than firing.

If you are attacked, you may experience this terror. The way you react to it will determine your fate, so you had better react properly and promptly. The shock will hit you hard and affect your thinking.

A partner and I were working our way along a river in a very remote region of Alaska. There were no signs of any human having been in this area for at least 50 years. We did find some very old human remains, and that was the only way we knew a person had ever been there before us.

It was raining and cold and the going was tough. Near evening the rain subsided and we stopped for the night to eat and dry out. We got a nice hot fire going in a dry wash and pitched our tent among the trees up on the bank. The coffee was perking, my boots were off and I had a pot of water boiling in preparation for cooking supper. My rifle was leaning against the bank of the rocky gulch in which we had built the fire, about 20 feet away from me. I was not wearing a sidearm.

I knew I should have had my rifle right beside me. We had seen signs of a mad bear for a couple of days now. He was ripping trees apart and clawing up the ground. Worst of all, the bear was following us. From the size of the broken trees, we knew he was a fairly hefty fellow. More than once I looked over at my rifle and said, "I've got to get up and get that rifle." I was warm though, my boots were off and I was sipping a cup of hot coffee.

My partner went to the tent and I asked him to bring my rifle to me when he returned to the fire. About 35 feet separated us at that point. I never heard a thing. I had just put my coffee down and was adding some salt to the pot of boiling water. Just by chance, and purely by chance, I glanced up. Coming full tilt right at me was the grizzly.

I have no recollection of that next instant, although I did become airborne and fly across the fire, because we found the salt container a good 20 feet from the fire. Standing by the trees, my partner's line of fire was blocked. I reached my rifle and whirled to face the charging bear right behind me. The bear evidently had broken his momentum to come down the bank into the gully. That pause saved my life.

I experienced the shock I described earlier—an almost overpowering awe at the ferocity of the animal. Had I not become combat experienced in Vietnam, I might have succumbed to that shock for a critical instant and the bear would have had me. I pulled the trigger and the .300 Winchester Magnum hit the charging animal squarely. The shot shook the bear and slowed him for a second, but he kept coming. I slammed another round in the chamber and fired again. The 220-grain slug hit him squarely again at point-blank range and knocked him back. I fired again and his body shuddered, but he still wasn't down. His gaze was locked on me as we faced each other, so close. The bear charged me once more. I leaped away, feeding rounds from my pocket into the rifle, and fired repeatedly.

The grizzly began biting at one of his bullet wounds but kept coming. I shot again and finally knocked him down, but he came right back up. By now my partner had joined the fight and was blasting away with his rifle. I dropped back farther. The bear ignored my partner, but strove to get me as though he had radar. I shot him again and finally turned him. He leaped up the bank and into the brush, still trying to reach me by running parallel to the gully.

All we could see was that swaying, crackling brush. My partner crammed another magazine into his rifle and sprayed the bushes. I ran to my pack, pulled out a box of cartridges and put some shots after him, but the bear retreated. The fight was over for the moment.

We put our boots on, loaded up and gave chase up the mountain. Catching a glimpse of the bear watching us from a stand of pine, I fired again and he fled. I hated to leave a wounded animal, but the visibility was bad in the forest because of the overcast sky. My partner and I began making our way back to camp.

The bear, we soon discovered, was following us. Once at camp, we prepared for a long night and another attack. We built up the fire, put on a pot of coffee and laid out our ammunition, ready for the grizzly.

The attack never came. The bear did come close once more, but we could not get a good shot. Firing a round in the air kept him at bay. He died of his wounds during that night.

We never figured out the reason for the attack, other than that the bear was deranged. Had I been completely unarmed when he attacked, I might have made it to a tree. Had the bear not been forced to break his momentum by descending into the gully, he would have had me. Had I not made a habit of always keeping extra cartridges in specific pockets and within easy reach, he probably would have had me.

The second incident occurred in the Yukon Territory. Another partner and I were driving along a bumpy old wagon trail, admiring everything. The forest was beautiful. It was late spring and some snow was still on the ground. We spotted an interesting stream and stopped to have a look. Neither of us bothered to get a rifle from the trunk of our car. We wandered into the timber about a quarter of a mile upstream, looking at rocks and plants. At the same time we were poking up the stream, a grizzly came poking down. We suddenly came face to face, shocking all three of us.

There wasn't a tree handy to climb, so we just started backing off. If we bolted and ran, the bear might be induced to give chase, so we kept our pace steady and smooth. This must have aggravated the bear because, with about 50 yards separating us, he began running at us. Something had to be done, or my partner and I would be goners. There would be no second chance.

This bear was young, so we tried a daring maneuver: my partner and I charged the bear! Screaming and waving our arms, we ran right at him. The bear stopped running at us and veered off. We continued our steady retreat once again. The bear started running back and forth in the woods about 100 yards from us, obviously agitated but unsure about what to do. Once again he charged, but his attack was not certain, so we again countercharged and again the bear retreated. He prowled back and forth and growled up a storm. We retreated faster, but 50 yards from the road the bear attacked again—and there was nothing uncertain about it. This was a vicious, determined bear. We measured distances and thought a sprint to the road might work.

The bear had farther to go than we did, but he closed the gap quickly. We flew onto the road with our legs pumping away. I jumped into the passenger's side of the car and slammed the door in the bear's face. The window had been open, and the bear leaped up and thrust his paw through it. I slid to the other side of the seat and onto my partner's lap while the bear's paw, just inches away, strained to reach us. I picked up a screwdriver and stabbed the paw as the bear was trying to force his head into the car. He backed off and we drove away.

Of course, I have been in other tight spots and have had fights that would make much better reading. I chose these two incidents, though, because they're good examples of bear encounters. The first illustrated the ferocity and determination an attack can have; the second illustrated an unarmed bluff that worked. But you must realize one thing about our actions during the second attack: We finally gave up and ran only because there was a place of safety that we could reach in time. To just turn and blindly run when confronted by a bear is the worst move you can make. You *cannot* outrun a bear. Many men have tried. There are ways in which you can *outmaneuver* a bear, however, which is what you must strive for.

One situation exists where you may be able to outdistance a bear while on foot, and that is going downhill. A bear cannot descend a steep grade quickly. He must go slowly, or his back seems to come right over the front, making him tumble. A bear can run up the side of a mountain at an unbelievable speed, but he cannot run down nearly so fast. I keep this in mind when traveling unarmed, and if I'm on a high ridge, I stay close to the edge to leap over the side in an emergency.

The bear is also an excellent swimmer. I once watched a grizzly swim into our camp across a fast current, maintaining a fairly straight line the whole way. A man in the water may get away from a bear if he were to swim underwater or leap into very swift water and let the current sweep him away. I don't think the bear would follow into the swift rapids. I have heard of men down on the Kenai Peninsula traveling unarmed through thick bear country and using just the rivers as escape methods.

If you run into a nonattacking bear, which is the more likely type of meeting, you may be able to scare him away by waving your arms and yelling. This is more effective on black bears than on grizzlies. If I were unarmed and started waving my arms at a grizzly, I'd want a tree nearby just in case. Remember, the grizzly is the top-of-the-line predator and in the wilderness he has probably never seen a human. He's accustomed to going where he wants without anything blocking his way.

Sometimes you can avoid a bear by crossing to the other side of the river. The bear does not have good eyesight, but he has a keen sense of smell. If you're downwind you may pass unnoticed even though the animal is within your view.

Some say that a grizzly cannot climb trees. Baloney! A bear can climb trees. If time permits you to be selective, pick a tree with trunk and branches thin enough so that the bear cannot get a grasp and pull himself up, yet stout enough so that the tree doesn't break under your weight. In an emergency there won't be time to be selective, but if you see a bear slowly approaching, you may want to climb a tree and let him pass.

It is a joke among miners that there's really no sense in carrying a firearm as protection against a bear, because the one time you neglect to have it with you is the time you'll meet Mr. Grizzly. This statement really means that you must never drop your guard. Never become so engrossed in what you're doing that you don't keep looking around you.

A friend and I were once felling trees to build a raft and float downriver to a village. We each had a rifle within quick reach at all times. I let my guard down for a moment and wandered away from my rifle to look for timber suited to our raft. I got farther and farther from my weapon and my partner. I had just felled a tree and stood back to watch it fall while leaning on my axe. I glanced over my shoulder and sitting a short distance away on his haunches, just watching the tree fall, was a bear.

Incidents like this occur often; you may just bump into a bear and sometimes it does seem as though it always happens when you are the least prepared. So be prepared! When you stop for the night, sleep next to a good climbing tree. While you walk, be aware of the threat of a bear and keep your eyes open. Stay close to the river in case you need a quick exit. If you come across an old cabin, pick up a pot and a spoon and bang them together. This technique is only marginally effective, but it is slightly irritating to the bear that may be denning inside and may cause him to leave.

Don't believe that just because you're a human and he's a wild animal, he's naturally afraid of you. Many animals that have never seen a human can be approached to within a few feet. That bear has no fear of you; many of the methods used to frighten a bear in the Lower 48 are only marginally effective in the wilderness.

I'm not certain if fire is an effective deterrent. I have seen cases where bears were not afraid of a campfire and I have seen other cases when they were. I once held a huge grizzly at bay all night with the aid of a fire. It was late fall and the night was black, making a good shot impossible. I spent the night by a large fire, and whenever the bear got close I fired a round in the air.

I know that animals leave the woods very quickly during a forest fire, so a fire must have some effect. I usually keep a pile of the dead, lower branches of a spruce tree right beside the fire so that if the occasion arises I can throw these highly flammable branches on the fire, making the flames go high.

I feel that very few bear attacks are unprovoked. The person experiencing the attack may not be aware of what he did to provoke it, because it's possible to trigger an attack without ever knowing you irritated the bear. One such situation occurs if you come across cubs. You may not even realize they're in the bushes beside you, but your presence is one of the most motivating situations a bear can experience.

If you see a bear cub, do not even take a split second to look at it for curiosity's sake. Get away! Run, but look around you while you do and prepare for the attack by staying near climbing trees.

The grizzly has a habit of allowing a kill to decay before consuming it. I have seen these kills. The bear throws leaves and sticks on top of it so that it's partially covered. If you find one of these kills, act as though you had found some cubs. If the bear is at the kill, you may be viciously attacked. A grizzly becomes extremely irate if disturbed while eating.

When you kill an animal and have taken whatever meat you want from it, do not return unarmed to that kill for more. Camp beyond the kill so you won't have to walk by it when you leave.

While prospecting I once mined the ground of a man who had been terrified of bears all his life. One day he killed a moose and was packing out the meat. When he returned for another load of meat, a bear was there and killed him.

If you are unarmed, don't clean fish and leave the entrails where you're sleeping. Don't stumble through brush where your vision is obscured. Many bears are motivated to attack because they are completely surprised by the human.

Do not underestimate the Alaskan black bear. He in no way resembles the garbage can black bears you see begging for food in the national parks. In Alaska and the Yukon, this bear is bigger than many grizzlies you see in zoos in the Lower 48.

There aren't too many attacks by black bears, but in the wilderness they're surely nothing to scoff at. If you happen upon a cub and are attacked by the mother, you will be facing a large, formidable animal. I have met several Alaskans who felt the black bear was more prone to unprovoked attacks and less predictable than the grizzly. I don't agree with this belief, but there do appear to be more black bears than grizzlies and you're more likely to encounter a black bear than a grizzly. Most of my serious trouble has been with grizzlies, and the black bear seems to scare off more easily than a grizzly. But make no mistake—a black bear can be very dangerous. I know of an incident where two armed men were killed by one black bear near an area I have prospected. This occurred in plain view of a group of their friends, none of whom could reach them in time.

The one and only thing that will protect you from bears is common sense. Be vigilant and use common sense as you travel.

Outdoor Life, October 1982

Last Day of the Wardens

BY JIM ZUMBO

Idaho conservation officers Bill Pogue and Conley Elms
thought they were making another routine arrest.
Then a desert trapper cut loose with his revolver.

Bill Pogue

Conley Elms

*Editor's Note: This story was obtained from interviews with various law-
enforcement officials in Idaho, including state Fish and Game officers, an
Idaho Bureau of Investigation agent, and the Owyhee County sheriff. The
accounts of the shooting and the events that followed were obtained from the
testimony of Jim Stevens, the only witness to the shooting, and others at an
Idaho judicial proceeding on February 3, 1981, the purpose of which was to
have Bill Pogue declared legally dead. A potato farmer from Winnemucca,
Nevada, Stevens has cooperated with enforcement officers, and several poly-
graph tests indicated he was telling the truth.*

It had been a long trip for Idaho conservation officers Bill Pogue and Conley Elms. After a five-hour, 175-mile drive across the rugged desert near the Idaho-Nevada border, the wardens finally parked their pickup at 3 a.m. and crawled into bedrolls.

They slept only a few hours on that morning of January 5, 1981. Both rose at dawn to meet with a rancher who had reported illegal trapping.

Nearby, 30-year-old Claude Lafayette Dallas Jr. was camped along the south fork of the Owyhee River. An experienced woodsman, crack shot, and survival expert, he was said to be running 80 traps in the area, mostly for bobcats. A self-styled mountain man, he reportedly took what he wanted from the land without regard to game laws. Dallas was not fond of game wardens. A few years earlier, when arrested in Nevada for a game violation, he'd told law-enforcement officers that he'd never again be taken into custody.

As the morning progressed, Pogue and Elms questioned the rancher. He told them he had ridden into Dallas' camp on horseback a few days before and had seen bobcat hides and fresh venison hindquarters. Deer season was long past, and the Idaho bobcat season hadn't opened. Dallas was in a hostile mood, and the rancher sensed his life was in danger, thinking he might be gunned down before he left the camp. The rancher warned the wardens to be extremely careful.

REWARD
UP TO
$20,000

For information leading to the Arrest and Conviction of

CLAUDE LAFAYETTE DALLAS, JR.
for the Murder of two Idaho Fish and Game Officers on January 5, 1981.

- Date of Birth: 3-11-50
- Height: 5' 10"
- Weight: 180 lbs.
- Brown Hair (may be shoulder length)

- Brown Eyes
- May have full beard
- Wears glasses
- Social Security No. 270-49-0296

Subject is an accomplished trapper and shooter.

SUBJECT IS ARMED AND EXTREMELY DANGEROUS.

CONTACT —
Sheriff Tim Nettleton, Owyhee County, Idaho - Murphy, Idaho 83650 — (208) 495-2441

Authorities sent this poster throughout the West.

In the meantime, Nevada potato farmer Jim Stevens was making the long overland trip to visit Dallas on that same day. Dallas had worked on his farm. Stevens anticipated spending a few days relaxing and helping with his friend's chores.

The following account is based on Stevens' description of what then took place.

Before heading into the Idaho desert, Stevens stopped at the Paradise

Bar in Paradise Hill, a tiny Nevada town north of Winnemucca. He picked up Dallas' mail and supplies from George Nielsen, the bar owner and a close friend of the trapper.

Nielsen lent Stevens a gun and told him to signal Dallas by shooting twice in the air from the top of a hill about three-quarters of a mile from the camp. Upon hearing the shots, Dallas was supposed to hike up the steep trail to help pack supplies to camp.

When Stevens drove to the rim above the camp and fired twice, he heard no answering shots. He decided to walk in with some of the supplies and met Dallas walking up the trail. After they greeted each other, Stevens continued to camp while Dallas went to the vehicle for the rest of the supplies.

Dallas' camp was a white, 10 X 12-foot wall tent about 50 yards from the river. When Stevens reached it, he put the supplies down and went for a walk along the river. Sometime later, he heard voices from the direction of camp, and someone shouted for him to return to the tent. Officers Pogue and Elms were talking with Dallas.

Apparently the wardens had met the trapper on the trail or at the vehicle. Pogue had unloaded a handgun that Dallas wore on a belt holster.

When Stevens walked into camp, the wardens unloaded the gun he had borrowed from Nielsen and continued their discussion with

Scene of the shooting at Dallas' campsite.

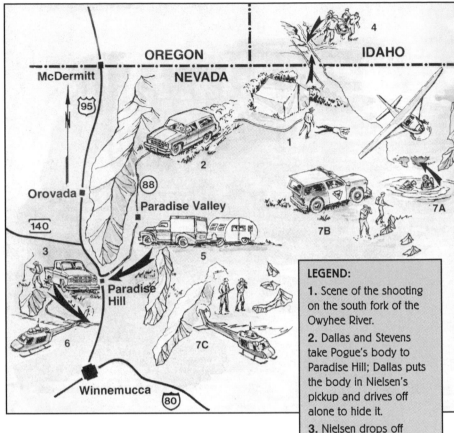

Dallas about the reported violations. At that point, one of the officers evidently saw a bobcat hide inside the tent.

Conley Elms entered the tent. "Here are the hides, " he said as he emerged with a bobcat pelt in each hand.

"Well, am I under arrest then?" Dallas asked.

"Yes," Pogue answered.

Bill Pogue, who had been an Idaho conservation officer for 15 years and before that a police official and game warden in Nevada, was known as a first-class warden, one of Idaho's best. He was outwardly stern, and had earned the nickname, "ice man with the steely eyes." A wary man, he always expected trouble. He watched Dallas intently, ready to draw his .357 Magnum at a moment's notice.

But, despite his training, instincts, and skills, he momentarily took his eyes off the trapper to look at the bobcat hides Elms was holding. Dallas drew a gun.

"Oh no!" Pogue exclaimed, and the next sound was the roar of the gun.

Stevens had been looking away from Dallas, and the blast startled him so badly that he almost jumped into the middle of the shooting. He turned just as Dallas fired a second shot. Pogue fell backward, and there was a cloud of gunsmoke and dust between Dallas and the stricken warden.

Elms had been crouching as he came out the tent. Dallas spun and shot him twice before the warden could reach his revolver. Pogue was still moving and had managed to get his gun out of the holster, but it fell to the ground. Dallas shot Pogue two more times. Then he went into the tent, came back out with a .22 rifle, and shot each warden once in the temple just as he would dispatch animals in his traps.

Dallas turned to Stevens. "Sorry I got you in this, buddy," he said. "You gotta help me."

Dallas waded across the river to catch two packmules he owned. Unable to catch the bigger mule, he returned with the smaller animal. It weighed little more than 300 pounds. While Dallas was gone, the frightened Stevens had reloaded the gun he'd carried, and he wondered if he'd be the next to die. Later Dallas took the gun and ordered Stevens to help.

The two men loaded Pogue's body on the mule and packed it up to Steven's four-wheel-drive. The Fish and Game truck stood nearby.

Conley Elms' body weighed about 280 pounds. The pair managed to load it on the mule, but the animal balked partly up the mountain and refused to continue. Dallas unloaded the body, used the mule to drag it back down to the river, and dumped the body in.

He and Stevens then destroyed as much evidence as possible. They poured kerosene on blood spots and the wardens' bloody clothing and burned them.

Then they drove to Paradise Hill with Bill Pogue's body in the back of the four-wheel-drive. While on the way, they concocted a story to clear Stevens of the incident.

The men pulled up to the Paradise Bar after driving several hours. It was about midnight when they arrived. Dallas knocked on the door of Nielsen's house and told him what had happened. He also said he wanted to use Nielsen's pickup truck to dispose of Pogue's body. Dallas told Stevens to remove his bloody clothing and take a shower. He told Nielsen to burn the clothing.

Dallas filled up the pickup's gasoline tank, moved Pogue's body into the truck, and headed out alone into the night. Stevens went home to Winnemucca, and Nielsen stayed at his home.

When Dallas returned later, he told Nielsen to take him to a drop-off point. Nielsen drove to a road 12 miles north of Winnemucca, turned west onto another road for two miles, and dropped off Dallas in the desert. The trapper had $100, an olive-drab duffel bag, a backpack, a rifle, and at least one handgun.

Stevens told his wife the false story he had put together with Dallas. His wife thought he was lying and confronted him. The shaken farmer confessed and agreed to go to the authorities with the truth. But before going to the police, he drove to Paradise Hill and told Nielsen he was turning himself in. Nielsen agreed to do the same. Together they told their story to an attorney and a county prosecutor in Winnemucca. No charges were filed against them either in Nevada or Idaho because law enforcement authorities are said to believe that both men acted under coercion and duress. Finally, by the afternoon of January 6, the pieces were fit together.

Since it was almost dark, searchers could do little until morning, but Tim Nettleton, Owyhee County sheriff, had time to fly over the camp area and he saw the Fish and Game truck. By daylight the next morning, about 30 hours after Dallas had last been seen, law-enforcement officers from several agencies had begun their search. The FBI was involved as well, because Dallas had crossed state borders.

Conley Elms' body was found in the river that first morning, about a quarter-mile downstream from the camp. But even though the wardens and police widened their search, they found no trace of Bill Pogue's body or of Claude Dallas.

Officers found the spot where Dallas got out of Nielsen's truck. The footprints led into the desert, then turned and came back toward the road, where the trail disappeared. Nevada's chukar season was still open, and hunters' tracks were mistaken for Dallas'.

An intensive week-long search failed to turn up Dallas or Pogue's body. Ed Pogue, brother of the dead warden, vowed to continue the search until his brother's body is found and Dallas is captured.

"Bill and I were awful close—as close as brothers can be," Ed Pogue said. "He was my only brother, and you can imagine how I looked up to him. Even after we grew up, we still made it a point to hunt together in Owyhee County."

Bill Pogue had many other admirers too. The 50-year-old senior conservation officer left behind a wife and four children. His family and friends knew him as a thoughtful, deeply sensitive man, despite his reputation as a gruff, stern, wildlife officer. He was an accomplished artist and enjoyed drawing scenes and persons associated with the outdoors. One of his pieces, which depicted a trapper and a wolf, appeared on the cover of *Idaho Wildlife* magazine, official publication of the Idaho Department of Fish and Game.

Conley Elms, 34, loved his job as conservation officer and had worked long and hard for the position. A wildlife graduate of Oregon State University, he never gave up trying to get a job as a conservation officer after moving to Boise with his wife Sheryl. He worked odd jobs at an electrical firm, a trailer factory, and with the Ada County assessor's office. After working part time with the Idaho Department of Fish and Game, his dream came true. He was hired as a full-time officer. To make his dream even better, his brother Michael was a conservation officer in nearby Mountain Home, Idaho.

This case is far from closed. As this issue goes to press, Pogue's body still remains hidden, and Dallas is at large.

Where is Dallas, and how did he escape the dragnet of searchers? No one has the answers. As one authority said, "Dallas could be at all points of the compass." When I asked Owyhee County Sheriff Tim Nettleton where Claude Dallas might be hiding, the tall, lanky officer took a deep drag off his unfiltered cigarette, shifted his weathered cowboy boots on his desk, and blew a thin stream of blue smoke toward the ceiling.

"Gut feeling?" he asked.

"Gut feeling," I answered.

"First of all," he said, "you have to understand he is capable of walking a long way over rough country, some 20 to 40 miles a day. My first guess would be he walked or got a ride to California where he's waiting for spring to break. Then he'll head for Canada where he spent time traveling in the past. "

This theory has strong possibilities, since Dallas was in the Northwest Territories with his brother recently and remarked he'd like to go back and run traplines.

"Since he learned the fundamentals of Spanish after working with migrant Mexicans on potato farms," continued the sheriff, "he might have headed south. He told some friends he wanted to go down there some day.

"He also might have headed for the swamps of the Southeast. His folks are in South Carolina, and the swamplands would be right for his style of living."

Nettleton showed me a map on the wall of his office. A pin was stuck in Paradise Hill. A string tied to the pin evidently had been stretched and rotated many times by frustrated officers as they tried to find Pogue's body. Because the police knew how many miles Dallas drove in Nielsen's pickup, they had the radius narrowed to 25 to 30 miles from Paradise Hill. Officers filled the gas tank afterward and determined about 85 miles had been covered, including the 25 miles Nielsen drove. That meant Dallas drove about 60 miles round-trip when he disposed of the body.

When Dallas returned to Paradise Hill, he said he hid the body where no one would ever find it. The region is pocked with countless abandoned mines and shafts, and he apparently found a place so perfectly suited that his boast was right. Despite a well-organized, methodical search and the assistance of psychics, Pogue's body is still hidden. Only Claude Dallas knows where it is.

And how about Claude Lafayette Dallas Jr.? What kind of man is he?

Born in Winchester, Virginia, he reportedly showed up in Nevada about 10 years ago, riding a horse and leading two packmules. Acquaintances say he rode west on horseback from the East.

According to Sheriff Nettleton, Dallas was clean and kept a tidy camp. He saw a dentist in Winnemucca regularly and did not smoke or drink. He had the ability to get along with people if he chose to do so. Well-liked in the Nevada farm communities where he worked, he was known to lend money to friends who were down-and-out.

"He wasn't a social recluse, either," the sheriff said. "He appreciated neons and nylons, if you know what I mean."

However, Dallas was considered unpredictable and dangerous by those who knew him.

"You don't dare cross Dallas," a friend told the sheriff.

Why would Dallas kill the game wardens? Evidently he felt they were imposing on his rights in the outdoors. Sheriff Nettleton explained that in Dallas' mind, the officers were trespassing in his domain.

Dallas has been formally charged with murder. Nettleton showed me three books discovered in Dallas' camp. One of them, *No Second Place Winner*, is about fast draw and firearms. A passage in the book says: "Be first or be dead—there is no second-place winner in a gun fight." Another book, *Kill or be Killed*, is described by its publisher in this way: "a book which belongs in every institution charged with the training of police officers or soldiers." The third book, *Firearm Silencers*, deals with various silencers used on weapons.

I asked the sheriff if he had any clues to Dallas' whereabouts.

"Not a thing," he said. "We get five or six leads daily, and we've checked every one out, but none were good. I'm afraid we might be in for a long search, maybe a year or more. Dallas will probably hide out in a big, wild area and he'll be tough to find. I just hope he doesn't gun down someone. I'm afraid that's how we might end up getting on to his trail."

Nettleton ground his cigarette butt into an ashtray, and for the first time his mood turned harsh.

"I want Claude Dallas," he said. "I want him bad."

And so do a lot of other people.

Outdoor Life, July 1981

Author's Note: Approximately sixteen months later, Claude Dallas was captured by the FBI. He was convicted in 1982 and sent to the Idaho State Penitentiary to serve a thirty year sentence. Dallas escaped from prison in 1986 and was captured a year later in California. Two years following his death, Pogue's remains were found in the desert.

I Went Whaling Alone

BY PHIL A. MOORE

My dory fairly leaped when I gave her the gun, then poised the harpoon. Along about then, things happened thick and fast.

Here is adventure—with a capital A! A veteran sportsman, who had tried every other known form of fishing or hunting, decided to go to sea alone in a small boat and harpoon a whale. What happened to him was—plenty! This is the most extraordinary story we have published in a long time and you'll find a thrill in every line.
—The Editor (1945)

Having hunted many kinds of big game, I have come to feel that, unpredictable though they are, one who is familiar with their habits when frightened or wounded is pretty well forearmed.

Besides, he has a powerful rifle to fall back upon. But harpooning a whale from a small boat—there was something I had never tried!

What would it be like? The very idea of approaching a whale and sticking it with a harpoon seemed a bit presumptuous; about like jabbing a boar spear into a rogue elephant. And why a whale will permit such familiarities was beyond my understanding. Perhaps the dumb beast does not savvy attacks from the surface of the water. Yet whalers tell us that whales that have been chased and stuck and have escaped do learn to be cautious—hard to sneak up on, also dangerous to boats which approach too close.

We have along the southern coast of Nova Scotia many sorts of whales, both large and small. The one most commonly seen in Mahone Bay is a saucy bold monster with a prominent dorsal fin. It's a grampus, according to local fishermen, and it may be a grampus sure enough. Or it may really be a pilot whale, for which "grampus" is a common misnomer. It's certainly not the white-splotched Atlantic killer whale, or orca, which those who've fished off Labrador also call a grampus.

When you see a whale only in the water, and never all of it at once, you can't examine it as you would a museum specimen; nor are you in any mood to do so! All I can say is that, unlike most Nova Scotia whales, our grampus has a mouthful of teeth, at least in its lower jaw, and, that the bigger specimens run almost as long as a tuna boat. Norwegian whaling skippers hereabouts (war refugees) call them "herring whales." For food they chase large schools of herring, mackerel, and squid, as do the giant tuna and swordfish of this part of the coast. If the fancy takes the brutes, they think nothing of plunging through the herring and mackerel nets, or tearing up miles of trawl. Accidents, of course, but the men who lose the gear say pure malice is to blame.

The fishermen are afraid of the big animals, for they do not scare easily and will smack right up against the keel of an anchored boat, or side-swipe it with a blundering tail. This does not happen very often, but often enough to make everyone aboard nervous when the grampuses get to feeding close by.

However, the urge to stick a whale with an old-fashion whaling iron kept digging at me. I knew it would be impossible, of course, to find one of those delightful little streamline cedar whaleboats, or an expert crew to row it. The best craft available would be an eighteen-foot Grand Banks two-man dory. With a clever boatman in the stern with a steering oar, and the harpooner standing in the bow, such a combination might work. I explained my project to several professional fishermen—and encountered a decided lack of interest.

"Monkey business, we calls it," was the way they expressed it. "And somebody is a-going to get wet."

Many of my fishermen friends cannot swim a stroke. Water to them is mainly a nuisance overlying the marine farm whence they take their crop of codfish. Otherwise it holds few attractions.

I soon gave up the idea of obtaining help from that quarter. But ways and means had to be found.

Among other small craft I have an eighteen-foot boat that is a Grand Banks dory forward and a hydroplane aft. It has a wide stern transom, and may be driven by any outboard motor with an extra-long shaft. Under the forward thwart is a ten-gallon pressure tank for gas. A pipe runs aft with a hose on the end and a valve with strainer. When I wish to fill the tank on the outboard, it is a simple matter to unscrew the filler cap, stick in the hose, open the valve, and fill her up. Three or four pounds of air pressure put in the supply tank with a bike pump will last a long time. A tire-tube nipple is soldered into the tank for this purpose.

The dory has a centerboard and also a sail. She is steered by an oar when under sail. She will plane when driven by a nine-horsepower four-cylinder motor, and can make fifteen miles an hour while carrying two passengers. The outboard consumes an imperial gallon of gas hourly. When turning, the dory will bank like a race horse, and come about in three times her length. In a heavy seaway she is all dory and as safe as a small boat can be. Steering lines extend from the tiller and pass through pulleys clear around the rail. You can steer from any position in the boat.

All this detail has a bearing on my whaling adventure; for I decided to use the craft in my plot against the whales.

For weapons I had a 100-year-old whaling harpoon and 100 fathoms of new nine-thread harpoon line with the inboard end fast to the mast step. Also I had an old whaling lance and 100 fathoms of new six-thread line attached to it—the inner end being made fast to a ring-bolt in the bow. The lance had a double-blade head shaped like a beech-tree leaf, and a four-foot shank fastened to a long pole or shaft. Such lances stab much more deeply into a whale than can a harpoon; and I intended to be fully equipped!

The next step was to try to find some adventurous soul with an active body who would handle the boat while I harpooned the whale. Finally, one guy promised to go, but when the time came to shove off, his wife refused to let him out of her sight. My own wife, long since used to my adventures, took the whole thing with her tongue in her cheek. But

"Don't you dare to land any smelly old whale on my beach," she warned, "or I'll just up and shoulder my pack and pull out for Times Square! Remember, now!"

At least she believed that I could catch a whale and come home to Chester alive. That was something!

I had a vague notion that if I could puncture a whale, it would tow the dory until it tired itself out, when I could pull up on it and stick it again with the lance and maybe kill it, or so wound it that my outfit would do the final towing. I could then take it triumphantly into the home port. Then what? Well, I did not know.

I felt a sneaking sense of relief when my friend's wife refused to let him go along. After all, this expected rendezvous with the whale was a personal affair. My friend had already asked a lot of questions about the enterprise I could not answer. They annoyed me. The only clear picture I seemed to have was of my boat, with me and my harpoon at one end and the whale at the other.

Practicing ashore with the harpoon, I found it heavy and awkward. The line weighed it down. It was also obvious that the line, when coiled in the boat, must not be behind me as I heaved the harpoon into the whale—if any. If I was between coil and whale I might get tangled in the whizzing line, and be drowned. The short distance I could cast the harpoon made it essential to run the boat practically up against the animal; and perhaps he would not permit such a near approach. Such were the problems that persisted in the back of my mind as I worked over the preparations.

When all was ready I headed out of Mahone Bay. The grampuses had been feeding in the shallow water between Owls Head Island and Southwest Island at the western entrance to St. Margaret Bay—the next bay to the east. The narrow inlet was about eighteen miles from Chester. Herring, squid, and mackerel often passed through it, and apparently the whales found it a convenient place to corner the schools upon which they fed. Making trips after tuna with sportsmen in the previous few days, I had seen several grampuses in water so shallow that their backs showed on the surface much of the time. They had paid little heed to our tuna boats as we trolled through the passage, steering clear of the powerful marine mammals in our anxiety to avoid a possible collision.

Now, as the boat and I skimmed along between the Seal Ledges and the mainland, several whales showed themselves. The water was shallow but there was too much sea room for my plans. Nevertheless, as one of those great masses of muscle slithered to the surface and spouted—quite near to my rapidly moving boat—I could feel goose pimples crawling along my spine. My stomach felt hollow and pinched up. Being a right-handed harpooner, I realized I'd have to approach the quarry on the port side, so that when I cast the instrument the coil of line would be on the same side of me as was the harpoon. Anything might happen after that. The whale, when hit, might go under the boat; it might sound and sink me with its flukes. But I had already been over all that. As the dory sped into the passage I had to put what might happen entirely out of my mind.

And there was a whale lolling around directly ahead of the boat! I slowed down and ran up on it. It lazily sounded when I was but ten fathoms away. The water was so shallow I could follow its wake with my eyes. I turned and ran along the wake. The whale broached, veered, and changed its course with a flip of its mighty tail. I yanked on the tiller ropes and veered also. The whale surfaced and turned sharply to its right. This put me on the wrong side in case I should catch up with it. I turned the boat to starboard. Again the whale veered before I could run alongside, this time to port. I overran.

This dodging about kept up for some time. But the whale could not go far, as the proximity of the land and shallow water forced it to turn. I am not sure the beast was aware that it was being persistently followed. It did not hurry or act as though frightened. It did not make for either of the outlets to the narrow channel. But it did suddenly disappear. For ten minutes or more I could see no sign of my quarry.

I had about given up hope when I spied its fin right near the high cliff known as Owls Head Island, which marks the northern or inner end of the passage into St. Margaret Bay. There against the cliff the water was some twenty fathoms deep. I steered away from the whale and maneuvered until I could approach from the bay side, and thus drive it back into the shallow water of the passage. Moving at about six knots, my boat and I approached the lolling monster. When about ten fathoms away, I picked up the harpoon and gave the engine the gun. The dory fairly leaped straight at that whale! I twitched the tiller rope to avoid running right up on its back, then poised the harpoon.

Things happened so fast from then on I cannot describe them. I have a memory, a mere impression, of a huge mass of unpredictable muscle suddenly appearing alongside. I slammed the razor-sharp harpoon into the middle of this mass.

The ocean exploded. The boat gave a lurch and was violently thrown sidewise, and all but tipped over. I caught a glimpse of curling flukes hanging over my head as I grabbed for a thwart and hung on for dear life. The line was sizzling out over the bow. I scrambled aft to give the boat a chance to turn if the whale turned, then grabbed the tiller itself and also slowed down the engine. The boat had been running as wild as the whale.

After a few seconds I could determine the course of the whale, by where the pull on the harpoon line was coming from. The animal had headed back into the passage and seemed to have taken a through ticket for the wide Atlantic. The line came at last to its end. The boat was yanked ahead with a powerful jerk. The bow almost went under. I speeded up the engine and this relieved the strain. The water was not deep enough for the whale to sound straight down, and wouldn't be for several miles. Thus it could not sink the boat—not yet!

What sort of whale it was, I couldn't even then be sure. I'd had it in mind to try for a grampus, as I've said; but this fellow—what little I'd seen of him—looked even bigger than I'd bargained for. For all I could tell, I might have tied into one of the smaller finbacks—a pike whale, or least rorqual. And those babies (if you can call them babies) run up to thirty feet or more! Anyway, that animated tugboat was giving me other things to think about right then.

I judged I was being towed along at about fifteen miles an hour—about the speed the boat could do by itself. So I cut out the engine and let the whale do all the work. As we went out of the southern end of the passage, the whale surfaced and spouted. The sun was shining and I thought I saw blood in the steam. I grabbed my camera and made ready for the next time the whale breached. I hoped to get a picture of the animal as it rode a wave and spouted. But each time I tried to stand up the whale would give a yank, and I would sit down with a bump. All I succeeded in getting were pictures of the sky or ocean, or of the line cutting the water ahead of the bow.

I had stuck my "fish" about 3 p.m. By sunset we were some five miles east of Chester Ironbound Island. The whale had settled down into a steady zigzagging swim toward Ireland—some 2,000 miles away. It was now going only about five miles an hour. Just about nightfall the sea began to make in a southwest wind. It got sloppy. The spray was heavy. I had to bail every once in a while. There was no let-up in the whale's power, but it kept changing its course.

The line came at last to its end, the boat was yanked sharply ahead, and I speeded up the engine to relieve the strain.

A long and ugly shark paddled by my boat. Its dorsal fin was about a foot above water. It gave me a grin as it passed. The whale was bleeding from the harpoon wound. The shark, following the trail of blood, passed on up ahead toward the whale. In another few minutes another big shark put in an appearance. It too looked me over. Its dorsal fin appeared to be about a foot and a half high. Either it was a lot larger than the first shark, or the phosphorescent wake made it seem longer. Soon along came another. As it grew darker, and I became more lonesome, those fins got bigger!

I did not like the situation. Those hungry lads looked very much longer than my little dory; and they took too much interest in me and my whale. One's imagination gets to working when one finds oneself alone, way out in an indifferent ocean—and hooked to a sea monster, with other monsters hovering about, seemingly awaiting eventualities. As yet, I had no idea of what that whale would decide to do, once it became bored with me and my dory. By 10 o'clock that night I could hardly see Ironbound Light. The whale seemed as fresh as ever. The ocean sparkled with eerie flashes of phosphorescence, made by those darned sharks—or I thought it did.

My enthusiasm for towing a whale into port dwindled. I was getting a long way from home. I was tired of talking to the whale, and of cursing the sharks.

At this point the towline went slack. The boat lost headway and wallowed in the sea. What now? Had the line parted? Was the whale doubling back to look me over? I soon got the answer. Almost alongside the sea erupted once more.

The dory gave a dangerous lurch. There was a whoosh! The top wave came into my lap; I could see a mass like a vast dark tidal wave almost over my head.

By some magic the dory slid out and away from this menace. There was a jerk of the line, and the dory tilted, all but buried her bow, then went swishing through those seas like a runaway torpedo! Then again the line went slack. Meantime I had started bailing as fast as I could, for the dory had shipped a lot of water.

Again the whale—or maybe a different one—leaped clear of the water. It was but a short distance ahead. I caught its huge menacing bulk against the sky as we settled in the trough. The thought raced through my mind that the monster was acting up the way a salmon sometimes does when, finding itself tired and unable to break away from the line, it will rush madly about and jump repeatedly in an effort to shake the hook.

But there was this difference: I could hold on and laugh at the salmon, whereas all the whale need do was give me just one good bump, or a slap with its flukes, and it would be good night for the fisherman—and no foolin'!

The line gave a jerk and again the whale went racing away, my dory hanging on and keeping on top as best it might. I bailed and cursed and prayed . . . and bailed and bailed.

Another whale whooshed right alongside; that did it. Too many whales!

The sea was choppy—and wet. I was fatigued with bailing, wearied with whales. I picked up the hatchet, went forward and cut the line, then gave the engine a spin and headed back for Chester. The wind was astern and the binnacle aglow.

In thirty minutes I again picked up Ironbound Light. It was a welcome sight. The dory spun along like the great craft she is, tossing the spray aside with the disdain of a first-class boat. She would wallow between two waves, take a breath, shoulder into the crest, then shoot like a rocket as she ran the rollers toward the home port. It took three hours to make the Chester landing, and I figured I had cut loose from Mister Whale and chums when some forty-five miles from home.

Yes sir, I now know exactly how it feels to navigate impudently up to a whale and practically stick my finger in its starboard eye! So what? Well, if you are looking for excitement, go out alone and try it. In the night.

And my wife? I switched on the light in the boudoir.

"Did you get the iron into it?" she yawned, one eye peeking from beneath the blankets.

I nodded.

"You decided not to bring it home with you, eh?"

"Right," I agreed.

"That's good," she sighed, and went back to sleep.

Outdoor Life, March 1945

A Lion Mangled Me

by John Kingsley-Heath

Back in camp, Kiebe (left) and one of the camp staff display fangs of lion that savaged me.

Our leopard bait was an impala we had shot and hung in an acacia tree on the edge of a dry river bed. It had ripened in the hot sun for three days, long enough so that we were sure if there were leopards in the country they could not resist it.

We had hung a number of baits, including zebra, gazelle and impala, but for some reason Bud Lindus and I both felt that this was the one that would get us what we hoped for.

The time was August of 1961. I was on safari with Lindus, his wife Pamela, and their 14-year-old son Roger, along the Ruaha River in the semiarid desert country of central Tanganyika. A retired oil salesman from Honolulu, Bud rates African hunting very high, and Pam and the boy share his enthusiasm for it. Bud and his wife were old clients of mine.

The foremost object of this hunt was a really good trophy lion. Two years earlier Bud and I had been led up the garden by a big-maned male, in the Kajiado district of Kenya. That one seemed to have the uncanny ability of disappearing at exactly the crucial minute, whether we approached him on foot or by car. He hid in the day, ate our baits at night, and, try as we did, Bud never got his sights on him.

He had come back to Africa this time determined to do better. Buffalo and kudu also were on his list, he wanted a good leopard for his wife, and if we came across an elephant with satisfactory ivory we didn't mean to turn it down.

We had sharpened our hunting senses on buffalo in the thick bush country of northern Tanganyika before moving down to the Ruaha River. Two buffaloes had got within a yard of us before going down permanently. After that we felt we were ready to take on most anything, including the biggest lion in Tanganyika if we could find him.

Our camp had been made on the bank of the Ruaha, under acacia trees that spread like huge green umbrellas. Thousands of sand grouse watered in front of the tents every morning. The wingshooting was wonderful.

Alvin Adams, a friend of Bud's from the States, had come out to join us for a fortnight, wanting a big leopard, and was hunting with Kevin Torrens, the second white hunter on the safari. Our numerous leopard baits were hung partly in the hope of helping Al get his wish.

Bud and I hunted lions, elephants, and kudu for days with no success. Tracks and signs were plentiful but we couldn't come across anything of the sort we were looking for. Leopards refused to touch our baits, and we began to wonder whether our luck was in or out. But when we hung the impala in the tree at the edge of the river two or three miles from camp, I had a hunch we were going to get action.

Bud, Pam, Roger, and I came into camp for a late lunch the afternoon of the third day after that, and when we finished our sandwiches and tea I suggested we go have a look at the bait. It was time for things to be happening if they were going to.

We drove out in the hunting car, taking along two gunbearers and trackers, Kiebe and Ndaka. Halfway to the leopard bait, however, I sent them off to follow some elephant tracks, with instructions to rejoin us near the bait tree.

We drove the hunting car to within 600 yards of the tree, then walked carefully the rest of the way. One peep around a large bush told us that a leopard had taken his fill. It was late afternoon now, almost time for him to return for his evening meal. There was not a minute to waste. We'd sit for him at once.

It was decided that Pam should have this first chance. Bud and Roger went back to the car to wait. Pam and I stole carefully up behind a thick bush and secreted ourselves in the bottom of it, first making a little hole for our guns.

Pam was carrying a rifle of European make, as light as the Tanganyika game laws permitted, for the sake of minimum recoil, mounted with a 4X scope. Mine was a Winchester Model 70 in .300 Magnum with a 6X Kollmorgen scope. Neither of the guns was right for what was going to happen, but there were good reasons for choosing them.

Sitting up for a leopard can be on the sticky side, especially if you are not used to it, since you know that if you fail to make a clean kill you have one of the most dangerous animals in Africa to deal with. Pam made no secret of the fact she was nervous. Unless the cat fell dead at her shot, she asked me to back her by putting another into him immediately.

That was why I had brought the scope-sighted Winchester. A 6X scope may seem unusual for a job of that kind, but it has its advantages. To begin with, it enables you to increase your distance from the bait, and often you can select a better spot by moving off a bit. Also, a leopard almost invariably comes on a bait late, when the light is failing fast, and the more powerful your scope the better its light-gathering ability.

Had my two gunbearers not been off following the elephant tracks, I'd have had one of them with us with my .470 Westley Richards double, but I couldn't very well manage to handle two guns by myself.

Pam and I made ourselves comfortable, with our rifles trained on the spot where we expected the leopard to appear. For 20 minutes nothing happened. The silence of late afternoon was settling over the bush. Puffs of wind blew through the acacias, stirring up little dust devils, but the breeze was from the bait tree, so we had no worry on that score. Now and then a bird twittered, and the shrunken river whis-

Morning after mauling, Dr. Brian McShane looks on as I start trip to hospital.

pered around its sand bars. Save for those small sounds, nothing broke the stillness.

It was an uneasy quiet, and as the minutes dragged on I began to be suspicious. Something wasn't quite right. Was the leopard approaching from behind us? Had he scented us and slunk away? We tried to keep a sharp watch all around, but there was no movement in the brush or grass. The time ticked off and my uneasiness grew. Then, suddenly aware of movement or noise behind my right shoulder, I turned my head ever so slowly and I was looking a huge maned lion in the face, just 20 feet away.

The whole situation was clear in a flash. The leopard had not come to the hanging bait because the lion had kept him away. The lion couldn't reach the impala himself. (A lion can get only about 12 feet off the ground on a very thick, sloping branch, but a leopard can run up one about three inches thick.) Now, hungry, disappointed, and angry, he had spotted us in our thick bush, had not seen or smelled enough of us to know what we were, and was stalking us for a kill. And he was close enough for that final, lightning-fast rush with which a lion takes his prey at the last second.

When I turned my head and we stared into each other's eyes, he recognized me for man, but it was too late for that to make any difference. I saw his expression change from the intent look of a stalking cat to one of rage. His face wrinkled in a snarl and he bunched his feet under him for the spring.

It all happened a great deal quicker than I can relate it. One second I was staring fixedly at the leopard bait. The next I was looking the lion in the face, he was gathering for his leap, and I was swiveling my rifle around from the hip.

The eyes of the big cats, I think more than those of any other animal, mirror what is going on behind them. At the instant of attack those of a lion seem to be on fire. The burning yellow orbs of this big male blazed into mine, and there was no misreading their message.

I did not wait to bring the rifle to my shoulder. I was sitting on my hunkers, and I whipped it across my knees and pulled off at him, all in a split second, trying for the thickness of his shoulder. The shot struck a little too far back, but he reacted to the 180-grain soft-nose as most lions do to a hit, whipping his great head around and biting savagely at the wound.

Pam and I were not conscious, then or afterward, of running through the six-foot bush where we were hidden, but we did it, and never got scratched. We got clear and raced for the car. In the thicket behind us bwana simba was roaring and thrashing in pain and anger. We ran until we were far enough away to be safe, then stopped to get our breath and congratulate ourselves on a very narrow escape.

"We have to get this chap," I told Bud when we finished panting out the story. "You and I will have a lion war."

My two gunbearers were not yet back from their elephant scout. We left Pam and Roger in the car, and Lindus and I took our heavy rifles and hurried off. Mine was the .470, Bud's a .450/400 double made by Manton & Co., a London firm. Both were good lion guns, but because we had not expected to encounter a lion and had thought we might get a chance at an elephant that afternoon, we had only solid ammunition along instead of the soft-nose loads we would have preferred.

The lion had left the place where I shot him, and it was plain from the blood that he was reasonably well hit. The blood spoor led down to the bottom of the dry river bed. There, although he was bleeding heavily, it had dried in the sand and lost its color, making it difficult to follow in the evening light.

He had run for a way under the river bank, climbed a small gully, and had gone into a thicket of mswaki bush, an evergreen that grows like thick weeping willow, with the outer branches draping right down to the ground, leaving a cavelike opening underneath. The lion had left little sign on the hardbaked sand, and we went down on our hands and knees to track him through gaps between the bushes.

We didn't crawl far before I pulled up short. "This is no good," I told Bud. "If we go ahead with our eyes on the ground, we'll walk right down his throat. Kiebe and Ndaka should be back at the car by now. We'll get them and let them do the tracking while we watch over their heads."

Kiebe is a particularly good man to have along in a situation of this kind. A Kamba by tribe, he had hunted for 25 years, eight of them with me, and before that with Miles Turner, one of the most famous of East African white hunters. I had saved Kiebe's life a time or two, and he had saved mine. Tracking down a wounded lion is nothing new to him, and he is absolutely without fear. I knew I could count on him no matter what happened. The second tracker, Ndaka, was a stand-in, and he was willing and brave.

The two of them were at the car, and we hurried back to the place where we had left the lion track. It was lucky we had quit when we did, for 15 yards ahead we found the blood-stained bed where he had been lying.

He had moved about 30 yards into another thicket while we were gone, still bleeding. We tracked him foot by foot, with Kiebe in the lead. It was not a job any of us liked, but we had no choice. Once a hunter starts an affair of that kind it's up to him to finish it, no matter how sticky it gets.

Kiebe wiped warm blood off the leaves, and held up a hand to warn me we were getting close. Then the lion announced his presence with an angry growl from the mswaki just ahead, and we saw him shoot across a narrow opening into the next bush.

It was almost dark now and in a few minutes we'd have to give up. We left the track and circled, hoping to push him into the open, but nothing stirred and no sound came from the thicket. We wasted precious time, the light got worse, and at last I whispered to Kiebe in Swahili, "This is for tomorrow. We'll let him stiffen up and beat him out in the morning."

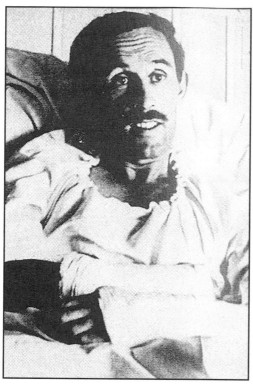
Two weeks later, I look worse than I feel.

The tracker's reply was a finger jabbed sharply to the left. There, under a low bush 50 feet away, the lion lay broadside, breathing heavily, watching us. I could barely make out the shape of his heavy body in the dusk.

The range was close enough, but we were shooting with open sights in very bad light and had to be absolutely certain of a hit. I took Bud by the arm without saying a word, and we shortened the distance to 40 feet, moving warily to the nearest tree, where a leaning branch would give us a rest for the rifles.

The shot belonged to the client, and since Bud was a first-class rifleman I did not expect there'd be any need for me to fire. But I made one bad mistake. I overlooked the fact that in the half-darkness the flash of his rifle would blind me for that critical fraction of a second when the lion might come for us in case Bud failed to kill him where he lay.

Bud's 400-grain solid took him in the shoulder a bit high, but because the bullet was not a soft-nose it went all the way through without opening up, doing only slight damage to the lungs. And in the instant when I should have hammered another into him I could see neither lion, thicket, or anything else.

He came in a rush the first few feet, then covered the rest of the distance in two great bounds. I had time only to yell at Bud to dodge behind me, when a huge ball of snarling fury landed at my feet.

I slammed a 500-grain solid into his head between the eyes, point blank, and, but for a fluke, that would have ended the affair. But, because he was badly wounded, when he hit the ground in front of me his head jerked forward and down, like a man who has jumped off a stool. My bullet struck him squarely between the eyes, as the hole in the skull showed later, but instead of going through his brain and leaving him deader than mutton, it passed down between his lower jaw bones and out the side of his throat, hardly more than blinding him with the rifle flash.

He leaped past me within a foot and lit between Bud and me, headed for Bud. I saw that Bud's rifle was tangled in branches and he couldn't get it down. The quarters were too close for a second shot without endangering him. I took one step and clubbed the lion on the head with the barrels of my .470 as hard as I could. He grunted, shook his head, and wheeled around. Before I had time to pull my second barrel, he pounced.

A quarter of a ton of growling, raging cat hit me full length, and I went down as if I had been electrocuted. It felt about like that, too. There was no pain and I was not stunned, but the shock of the blow as the lion crashed into me, with his forepaws over my shoulders and his huge body bearing me to the ground, was beyond description. My gun went flying out of my hands, and then I was lying on my back with the lion on top of me, his front legs wrapped around me and his paws under my shoulder blades.

A lion, even wounded, often pauses for a second after his initial leap has knocked his victim down, and this one did just that. That tiny pause saved my life. I knew that within a second or two he would bite me through the head, and I smashed my right fist into his nose with every ounce of strength I had. I broke the bones of the hand, but he opened his mouth at the punch, I suppose to growl, and I followed through. I rammed my fist down his throat, and his teeth closed on my arm halfway to the elbow.

I heard the bones crunch, but in a strange detached way, not as a sound from outside, but as if I were hearing the arm break from inside my body.

So long as I kept my fist down his gullet he could not get at my head or throat. I could feel his claws under me, ripping my sheepskin hunting jacket to shreds and my back with it. I knew that if he got his hind feet on my belly he'd tear my guts out with one rake. I twisted on my left side, drew my legs up to protect myself, and concentrated on trying to keep my arm in his mouth.

The statement has been made more than once that a man attacked by one of the big carnivores is overcome with a merciful numbness, so that he feels little or no pain or fright at the time, perhaps because the shock overwhelms his nervous system. I think the part about being benumbed is true, but for a different reason. The victim of such an attack is fighting for his life and knows it, and a man in that situation has little sense of feeling. Certainly, in my case, I felt very little pain through the whole mauling. When it was all over my back looked as if I'd been flogged with a cat-o'-nine-tails, but it didn't hurt while it was happening.

Nor did I smell the lion's breath or have any sensation of feeling his mane against my face, although I know it was there. I did have a bad bit of nightmare in the hospital later, when I felt his saliva all over my fingers and woke up in a cold sweat trying to get my mangled arm out of his jaws.

Actually, he took care of that for me. He shook me as a terrier shakes a rat, rolling me back and forth, and freed himself of my fist and arm as a big fish gets rid of a bait.

It takes far longer to describe such an experience than to live through it. Everything was happening at once. "Get my gun!" I yelled at Kiebe in Swahili. "Kamata bunduki yangu! Piga the bloody thing!" Piga means hit, but in this case I meant shoot and the tracker knew it.

Then I saw Bud come into sight over the lion's rear quarters and his .450 bellowed twice. But because I was lying under the cat he could only shoot far back. We learned later that he broke a hind leg, but the lion paid no attention, neither flinching nor turning its head. It just went on growling and mauling me, and took no notice of Bud, Kiebe, or Ndaka. That is typical lion behavior. Once simba gets his victim down he stays with it. A wounded leopard will rush from one member of a party to another, biting at the first man he can reach, then striking instantly at a fresh victim, only to leave that one and run for the next. A lion, however, takes time to finish what he begins.

Kiebe grabbed my gun now, checked swiftly to see which barrel was loaded, ran in, and shoved the muzzle against the lion's shoulder, heedless of his own danger. But from where I lay beneath the brute I saw that the bullet, whatever it might do to him, would also smash through my knees, and I screamed at Kiebe, "For God's sake, don't shoot there!"

He backed away a step and blasted the one round remaining in the

.470 into the lion's back just behind the shoulders. That put Kiebe out of the fight, for the rest of my ammunition was in my pocket under the lion. But the shot was strong medicine and well placed. It broke the spine, and the lion twisted off me. A wounded lion doesn't quit as long as he is breathing, however, and this one wasn't finished yet. Back he came for me on his front legs, with his back end dragging, and quick as I moved I wasn't quick enough to get to my feet before he was on me again.

He'd have taken me through the left side of the chest with his huge canine teeth, and one bite there meant certain death, but I threw up my left arm to fend him off. I had no time to jam it down his throat, as I had done with the right. I simply shoved it into his face. He grabbed and crushed it just above the wrist, and once more I heard my own bones break like match sticks, not as I would have heard another man's but as a noise coming from inside me.

At this point, Ndaka did a very brave thing. He threw himself on the lion and stabbed it again and again in the ribs and throat with a six-inch knife. Then Bud, who had been stuffing fresh shells into the breech of his double while Kiebe got in his shot, stepped close and sent two more solids crashing into the lion. The great body jerked and sagged and rolled off me.

As I struggled to my knees, half helpless from my broken arms, I jabbed my left foot into his face to kick myself away from him. That was the wrong thing to do, even with a lion breathing his last. His jaws closed on my shoe and he bit down, and for the third time I heard the crunch of breaking bones, in my foot and ankle now. And this time it hurt like hell! I wrenched my foot free, but the lion died with my shoe in his mouth.

We left him where he lay. We'd have to run the risk of hyenas tearing him up before morning. Bud and the natives carried me to the car and wrapped me in the rain curtains to keep me warm. Then we set off in the darkness for camp. There was no moon and we couldn't follow our tire tracks, so rather than get lost we stopped, made a fire, and let off a shot every 10 minutes. It's a rule on safari that if anyone fails to return to camp by an hour after dark, the search-and-rescue operation gets under way at once. We knew that by now Kevin Torrens, our other white hunter, was out looking for us.

My wounds had clotted well and I was bleeding only a little, but I drank water like a mad thing. Kiebe and Ndaka left us to try to find the way to camp, and shortly after that we heard the hum of a motor and then the lights of Kevin's Landrover appeared.

It was 2 a.m. by the time we found our way back to camp. Torrens cleaned my wounds, poured disinfectant into them, and I swallowed three times the normal dose of antibiotic tablets, washing them down with hot tea. Next, I got down two cups of soup and began to feel quite comfortable. But about that time I suppose I went into shock, for I started to tremble violently from head to foot and kept it up for hours.

We had a radio telephone in camp, but now it was Sunday morning (the lion had attacked me on Saturday evening) and the government radio in Nairobi was closed down, so Kevin left for the nearest phone at Dodoma, 120 miles away, 30 of it rough track through the bush, to call for a plane. We had scratched out a small airstrip near camp earlier.

Kevin got through to Peter Whitehead, manager of a leading Nairobi safari firm, at 6:15 on Sunday morning, and 45 minutes later Dr. Brian McShane, my physician and good friend, was air-borne and on the way with a supply of blood and the other things he needed to fix me up temporarily. Bill Ryan, another professional hunter from Nairobi and also an old friend, came along to take over the safari in my place. It was a 2½-hour flight. They touched down at camp at 9:30 that morning.

By that time I had sent our safari boys out and they had brought the lion to camp. The hyenas had not molested him. He was a magnificent brute, the biggest I had ever had a hand in killing, 10½ feet long and weighing 497 pounds. He must have weighed a bit above 500 alive, before he lost blood. There, in the Dodoma district, the lions live on buffaloes and the full-grown males are among the finest trophies in all of Africa. This one was paler than average, but not quite a blond, with a very heavy mane. As friends remarked later, at least I had been savaged by a decent lion, not one with just a ruff around its neck. Bud has the pelt, and I doubt he will ever take another trophy that will give him a more exciting time. He gave me a tooth and claw, which I have had mounted and use as paperweights.

Dr. McShane poured blood into me and set about patching me up for the flight back to Nairobi. I had two broken arms, a broken hand, a foot chewed and badly crushed, a horribly lacerated back, and a few deep holes in various parts of my body. As I was being carried into my tent after the attack, I had heard Kiebe tell the other safari boys, "Bwana ameliwa na simba" which is Swahili for the bwana was eaten by a lion. Maybe Kiebe exaggerated a little, but he was close enough to the truth so that I didn't feel like contradicting him.

I entered the Princess Elizabeth Hospital in Nairobi that afternoon, August 13, and stayed until October 2. I was on the danger list for a few days, but the surgeons repaired my broken bones and by great good fortune I escaped infection, which is very likely to follow an attack by one of the big cats because of their habit of feeding on putrid meat. The fact that I had been able to get down a massive dose of antibiotics a few hours after the accident probably accounted for my very good luck on that score.

The mauling proved far worse than the aftermath, and most of my stay in the hospital was not a bad ordeal, thanks in large measure to the efficient care of Dr. McShane. Bud and Pam were able to finish their hunt as they had planned, with Bill Ryan's help. They took a couple of fine kudu, and by the time they got back to Nairobi two weeks later, I was able to sit up and drink champagne with them, by way of celebrating my escape. I was well enough to leave on an easy safari the day I got out of the hospital, too.

For the courage he had shown, Kiebe received the Queen's Commendation for Brave Conduct a few months later. Asked what his thoughts were at the time, he replied matter of factly, "Do you suppose I am going to do nothing when a lion is about to kill my bwana? What would we do without him? We would have no safaris." And the only reward he wanted was corrugated iron to roof his house.

The following February I had the satisfaction of helping to whack another good lion in Kenya. I'm all for a lion war any time now, and I suppose I shall be the rest of my life.

There's an interesting sequel to the story. On August 12, 1962, a year to the day from the time the lion mauled me, I sat up for a leopard at that same tree and at the same hour. I had a lady client again, and we sat in the same bush where Pam and I had waited. The leopard put in an appearance as the light was starting to fade, my client fired, and the cat tumbled, hit hard but not dead. In the twinkling of an eye I now found myself in exactly the same predicament I had faced on that fateful evening a year earlier, except that this time I was dealing with a leopard rather than a lion. Not that that is much to be preferred.

It was too dark for tracking, so we went back to camp and returned the next morning. The blood spoor led into a bush nearby, and to my great relief the leopard lay dead there. So if there was any jinx connected with that tree it has been laid to rest. And one thing is sure. In all of Africa there is not another tree that I shall remember so vividly and long.

Outdoor Life, March 1963

Hurricane
Hunt

BY GERALD R. HUNTER

We knew the storm was stalking us, hunting the Florida coast just as we were. But it sprang suddenly, caught us as we ran.

I grabbed the anchor rope and tried to pass the end to Ed, floundering near by.

As a newsman here in south Georgia, I'm sure I get to see many more hurricane warnings than the average citizen.

I'm equally sure sighting one of these warnings on a teletype machine means more to me than to the average newsman. Each time I see one my mind races southward across the wire-grass flats and pine slopes of Georgia, across the cypress swamps and cabbage-palm hammocks of north Florida to a day when I punched a cash register instead of a typewriter.

I needn't mention the year. If you're an adult and read the newspapers or listen to the radio, you'll remember the incident before you read much farther. It was autumn, and I had just opened a sporting-goods store in east-central Florida. Considering my brief tenure, I had made a great many friends in the St. Johns valley, if one can think of so slight a depression as a valley. One of these new friends was Butch Newsom, a huge, lithe, tough, pleasant fellow of about 40 who knew the coast like the porch of his home. And I was to meet him this day, a September 17, the eve of my birthday. Many years have passed since birthdays meant much to me, as birthdays, but that date has leaped at me every year since.

In the grayness that should have been sunrise that morning, dark clouds sagged baggily over the very treetops, as if ready to split under their liquid weight.

Normally I wouldn't have seen this dreary vista. I'd have been asleep. But this morning an air of foreboding awakened me, and my little fishing barometer was already descending past the 29 mark. Aircraft known as hurricane hunters had for three days kept constant watch over what had become a monstrous cyclone centered near the Bahamas somewhere near my home in West Palm Beach. It was moving northwest, toward Jacksonville.

The storm worried me for two reasons: Hutch had offered to take me on a marsh-hen hunt this day, along with Ed Howe, a fat little Palm Beach insurance salesman. Second, a sizable crack somewhere above the main show window of my store was expected to admit a lot of water if it rained while the wind was easterly.

By noon the sky seemed lighter, but a fresh wind kept patches of dust swirling in the street. Sharp gusts under the rear door of the store scattered papers on my desk. I tested the ventilator windows for security, and spent a futile hour looking for the crack over the show window.

Hutch called at noon. "Everything ready?" he asked.

"Sure," I said, noticing through the window that people had begun to gather in little groups up the street, out of the wind, or to walk hurriedly about their business. "What about the weather?"

"Well," Hutch said, "looks sort of raw. But this wind will roll the water in like nobody's business, and you've got to have high tides to get marsh hens. Makes 'em flush easy."

During the time I'd been in Florida I'd never hunted marsh hens. I was anxious to try it. Still, I knew Hutch was venturesome. He was the kind of smiling, stubborn-chinned fellow who look as if he were afraid of anyyhing—and wasn't. Then I said, "That little bet I made about my average on these slow birds is hereby withdrawn, in this wind, but I'm willing to tackle 'em if you say."

"Storm warnings are out up to Cape Hatteras," Hutch answered, "but looks like we're going to miss most of it here." His deep bass voice was reassuring, and I said I'd expect him at 3 o'clock. It would take us nearly an hour to get across the causeway to Palm Beach and up the strand to the fish camp where we'd get the boat. Hutch had said we'd pole along and scare birds from the grass tops.

I didn't go home for lunch. I told my wife I was rushed at the store, because I didn't want her to talk me out of going. Actually, none of the clerks were busy. The only places doing any business were the coffee shops, and building-supply houses where customers were buying nails and sheeting to batten down against the blow. I ate a tasteless sandwich and kept going out to look at the clouds which still seemed lazy but which somehow passed quickly.

I called Ed, and he said he'd be ready if unwilling. All the time I kept remembering pictures of the Miami hurricane of the 1920's, of the huge ship blown ashore in Biscayne Bay park and stone houses reduced to the rubble you can still find in the lush weedery of Miami's suburbs.

Ed called back. Wasn't the hunt called off?

I told him no, that we still planned to leave at 3 'clock. When he demurred, I suggested he tell his missus he was going out to see a prospect, and promised to buy a $2 loss policy on one of my guns. Ed chuckled and said he was game, but his voice, already a little thin, seemed a little thinner. In addition to the storm, he was concerned about his wife who was overdue with their first offspring. Ed was the youngest of us, with a pink, round, Peter Rabbit face, and was surely no outdoorsman. But he'd said such a hunt would give him something fresh to talk about with prospective clients.

Just before 3 o'clock I called my wife again and told her I was going over to Palm Beach and wouldn't be back until after dark. That was indeed true, but I should have told her I was going hunting.

And why not? The storm wasn't coming anywhere near, and I'd been out hunting at all hours for years. Yet I had a little feeling of guilt. I dismissed it when Hutch pulled his Model A Ford up to the curb.

I threw in my waders, gun, two boxes of No. 6 shot, and climbed in. I almost asked Hutch to wait while I went back into the store to get a couple of life preservers; but then I decided I was getting all worked up over nothing.

At Palm Beach, Ed waddled out to the car with a raincoat, sou'wester hat, boots, moccasins, a huge hunting knife, a field coat, and about the worst stovepipe of a shotgun I'd ever seen. Hutch noticed me gawking at the gun, but he winked approvingly. "Ed's got the right thing for a salt marsh," Hutch said. "Spray and mist just eat up a good gun in no time flat. Took a fellow once who insisted on carrying a pretty automatic. Three weeks later we went on a deer hunt and he couldn't pull back the bolt. So we went back home an' I took it apart an' shook out enough salt crystals to churn up a jug of ice cream that same afternoon."

Hutch wasn't kidding about the salt. I thought of my nearly perfect Parker and was glad I had decided not to wipe off the heavy grease which had preserved it all summer.

As we drove up the strand north of the famous Florida resort, Ed worriedly kept looking up and down the sound. His chubby forehead was creased, and a sort of hunted look darkened his eyes.

"What's the matter, Ed?" I kidded, hoping to cheer him. "Got some poor insurance risks for the storm?"

"No," he said almost in a whisper. "It's just Lucy."

Lucy is Ed's wife. After a moment I said, "The hunt isn't that important. If you're worried about her and the baby, for heaven's sake let's go back. You don't have to be a nitwit just because Hutch and I are."

Ed slowly shook his head. "Maybe it is important," he said. "Nobody ever knows just what is. If talking about hunting marsh hens helps me sell insurance, it may be more important for me to be here than back at Palm Beach. I couldn't stop the hurricane, even for Lucy." His jaws were set as solidly as a tent rope in the rain.

I saw Hutch glance down at Ed, over the match he was chewing, and in Hutch's eyes was a new, surprised respect for the little man wedged between us.

The water in the sound looked different. Waves were larger than I had ever seen them and they seemed to carry farther. The crests reached from shore to shore in a steady, driving rhythm. They looked slow, but when they hit the steep inshore beach they pounded heavily, lashing high into the air, whipping over the lower part of the road. But Hutch drove on, humming a juke-box tune.

A mile short of the fish camp, the road hit a low spot where seas had once washed out the fill. It had never been properly rebuilt. Sea water was flowing across it. Hutch stopped the car, put on his waders, and carefully tested the depth. He seemed satisfied.

I wouldn't have tried it, but Hutch chugged right on through. The bottom felt shaky, and we stopped on the far side to see if a wheel on the chronically ailing vehicle might be loose. As we got out of the car there was a peculiar gurgling noise, and we saw the roadbed at the spot we had crossed dissolve in a sandy froth.

"Nothing to worry about," Hutch shrugged. "I think we can get through after the hunt, when the wind dies."

There was no other road. I looked at Ed, found him looking at me, hard.

At the fish camp all the boats were pulled out and staked down with their bottoms up. Kinley, the man who ran the camp, was boarding up windows and was surprised to see us.

"Bang-bang!" Hutch said, pointing his forefinger and clicking his big thumb. Hutch had known Kinley for years. "We want some meat."

"You mean you're going out in this?" Kinley asked. But he was already starting down to the landing where he took the lines off a 14-foot plywood skiff. I figured that was a pretty good endorsement of Hutch as a boatman.

When we put the skiff in the water, here on the lee-side of the strand, it lay as if in some farmyard pool. The water was unusually clear, and very low. Darting minnows scooted away. But I saw Ed was looking across the sound where even in the grayness we could see a mass of angry whitecaps.

"Hens all gone across by now" Kinley stated. "Nothin' doing on this side with low water. You got a good kicker, ain't you?"

Hutch took the little five-horsepower outboard from where he kept it clamped to the scarred door of the car. Kinley grunted. "Good lookin' little kicker," he said, but he seemed to emphasize the adjective *little*, as he looked from the motor to the whitecaps.

Straight across from the camp, a peninsula jutted out so that it was only about half a mile distant, but on each side of the shore the mud beaches swept away westward from the peninsula's weathered, sandy point. "Hadn't we better just go straight across to the peninsula, and work the shores from there?" I asked. "Then we could get ashore if the motor failed."

Hutch laughed. "Could. But wouldn't find no hens until we got to where the wind's piled the water up in the marshes, way over yonder." Watching Ed, he added, "We'll try it your way, though." Ed's face seemed a trifle blue, and the wind wasn't that cold.

Our trip across to the point wasn't bad. We pulled up into a creeklet and tied the boat to a mangrove bush. Spreading out across the finger of land, we began to wade through the scant marsh, hoping to kick up enough birds to persuade Hutch not to take the boat farther downwind. High tide ordinarily would have covered all but the grass tips here, but the wind had blown the tide up along the west shore.

Suddenly something flushed in front of me—a gray-brown bird whose speed increased rapidly. Hutch downed the bird as it angled toward him, retrieved the thing, and motioned for us to come look.

"The book says this one's a clapper rail," he explained. "There are at least three kinds of marsh hens: sora, the little bird they shoot in Georgia and Ca'lina; the Virginia that they shoot farther up the coast, and this one, the biggest of the lot." The bird was as large as a grown crow. Its flesh felt soft.

We started on, and suddenly a sharp gust of wind blew my cap off. I reached for it, and before I could get it on my head, it began to rain, tiny, stinging drops almost as fine as mist, blowing nearly parallel with the ground.

It became impossible to keep one's eyes open, traveling in the direction we had taken, and we reversed our course. On the way back toward the boat I bagged two birds and Ed missed an easy one. The rain grew heavy, drops becoming as large as buckshot.

Then, magically, the sun came out. Bright, hot on our necks where rain still trickled down. The rain stopped entirely, and the wind slackened.

We got back to the boat and were unloading our guns and thinking we had been fortunate to kill three birds under the adverse conditions, when the skies began closing in again with a blackness that suddenly turned the whitecapped water to ink and old lace.

Ed said abruptly: "I don't like it." He squinted as he looked back the half mile toward Kinley's camp, and when I followed his gaze I saw, creeping out from the shore, a massive series of ripples on the water that began to break upon themselves and throw spray into the air, hiding what looked like a figure waving wildly on the beach by the camp.

Hutch cast off. The boat drifted rapidly southwestward while he prepared to start the motor.

Ed called to him and pointed. When Hutch looked, the calm left his face. All at once it seemed leaner, and his morning whiskers stood out clearly. He pulled the starter rope and the motor roared dependably.

"She's gonna be rough when she first hits," he said, shouting now because the wind was a new force that flattened Ed's sou'wester against his forehead and, once, made a toot like a horn in my gun barrels. Hutch headed straight into the wind and opened the motor wide. It had a high-pitched, soothing whine.

The heavy sea had not yet reached us, and the little motor drove the boat steadily forward toward the landing. Nobody said "Guess the squall changed course." It was unnecessary. We all knew that, somehow, this was the first blow of the hurricane, the biggest in years, a capricious hurricane that had deserted its path to wreak unbelievable havoc on the Palm Beach area.

Our bow went up on the first wave with a lurch that threw Ed halfway out of his seat. He got busy and bailed. Several smaller waves passed, and we could see one ahead bigger than the first. Right then we felt a terrific jolt, probably a log floated off by the wind, and the quick scream of an outboard motor that has sheared a pin. Before Hutch chopped the throttle the boat broaching into the wind.

Ed grabbed an oar, but it was as if he were paddling with a toothpick. The boat was already broadside, and I heard myself yell: "Get another pin!"

Hutch didn't even look up from his flailing oar. "No wrench, no pins," he shouted. All of a sudden he dropped the oar and grabbed the gunwale. He was cartwheeling out as he shouted hoarsely, "Overboard!"

I didn't have to turn to know he was looking into the big wave. I grabbed the anchor rope and rolled out headfirst.

The wave hit just as I shook water from my eyes. I saw Ed, clawing at the buckles of his raincoat, pitched out of boat as it went up on its beam. The top of the wave slid under the boat, carrying Ed with it.

When the wave had passed I saw Ed swimming awkwardly, the chin strap of his sou'wester cutting into his throat, and I knew he was still trying to get rid of his coat. Hutch saw him too and yelled, but his words were lost in the wind.

The boat lurched and I stretched out my body toward Ed. I felt my foot bump him, and then he caught it and pulled himself within reach of the boat. I took a turn of the anchor line around my right hand and passed the loose end to him. It was slick and hard as a greased cable.

The boat was right side up again now, two thirds full of water. Hutch was working his way along the gunwale toward us when Ed began trying to climb into the boat. Hutch caught at him, pulling him back, and Ed was fighting him. "No good!" Hutch was shouting- "And get your clothes off—it's going to get worse!"

It did, almost before Ed got rid of his coat. The rain came again, blinding, choking, cold. Half of it seemed to be wind-whipped sea water, but I think that was because the boat's pitching kept me under the salt water half the time. Hutch got the motor unfastened and let it go before the stern sank.

The boat didn't sink though it got full of water and once turned completely over, but it pitched so it was impossible to hold on. We finally managed to get close together on the same side in the manner of an outrigger, constantly working to keep the boat upright, clutching each other and the rope. Once, with my head under water, I thought whimsically of my treasured Parker shotgun and Ed's old relic, and admitted mirthlessly that now one was no better than the other.

The rain increased, became a vertical river blotting out vision and sound until it seemed impossible to tell where the rain ended and the sea began.

Time passed. I couldn't guess how much. Finally I didn't even care, didn't care about anything except holding on so I could get my head above water part of the time. I sensed Ed and Hutch were still with me but I couldn't be sure, and I wondered about my wife and Lucy's baby.

I discovered I was seasick and must have been for some time. Horribly sick. Even through violent air maneuvers and a good many years at sea I had never known anything like this. Gasping for breath, I inhaled sea water and became sicker, if possible. But I held on, because I couldn't turn loose. I thought once, in a fleeting logical moment, that if I survived this my hands would show rope burns for weeks. Sometimes the rope would slacken, as if Ed had been torn loose; then it would tighten viciously with his weight, and seasick as I was I couldn't help thinking how bad it must be to be having a baby in a hurricane.

Once, or maybe it was twice, a bright sun shot through that awful rain. I was aware of its brilliance; I couldn't actually see it. Up, down, skidding sideways half underwater. Then over again, and over, and over again.

My legs? Something was beating on them and I wondered, with a moment of groggy horror, if they were numb and a shark or barracuda was at work.

Then there was pain. I kicked, mostly to see if they were still there, and felt something solid. I kicked again, and this time it tore the calf of my right leg. I extended a foot, and felt it dragging over something brittle and rough. It dragged for several seconds before reason came to me—oyster shells.

We were dragging over oyster shells, and the way we'd been drifting those could only be on the mainland shore, a wild, uninhabited salt desert that ran for miles along the sandy muck.

Then there were no more oysters. We were swept on again. My spirit died. And then—more oysters, higher this time, cruel, pleasant things cutting at my hips, banging my thighs. But at the speed we were drifting they would cut me to pieces! I made myself turn loose the anchor rope.

That was no better. Beaten about alone in that water, the shells would have killed me. But the boat overtook me, pounded at me as if asking me not to leave it. I mustered enough sense to crawl up on the gunwale. My weight pulled that side of the boat under water, but I lay half-drowned and thankful for the meager protection. I wriggled toward the stern and pulled a limp Ed partly into the boat too, even before I realized the boat was hung on the oyster bank. Ed had knotted the rope about his wrist. I found Hutch's legs under me, and then his face. The rain seemed a shade lighter, but it didn't matter, and I remember wondering if it was only Hutch's body I was holding.

We pounded on the shells. I knew, presently, that the bottom of the boat was nearly gone, and tried to protect my knees by lying over a thwart. The beating brought Hutch to life, too, for I suddenly found him helping me, trying to protect Ed. Then we were loose and drifting again, drifting into mangrove trees, pounding against their springy limbs.

The boat wedged fast. Hutch and I dragged Ed into the swamp until we bumped into a threshing palm tree. The three of us huddled in the torrential darkness with our backs to the palm, not even thinking of our cuts.

Then the body chemicals that had kept us fighting to live played out. We fell into nightmarish, exhausted dozing. We could feel trees crashing down about us, the sharp report of their cracking trunks piercing even the wind.

When I was fully conscious again I went through the torture of standing erect. Rain still fell, but now it was only a drizzle. The wind no longer shrieked. It was a fresh breeze under a gray dawn sky.

The palm was still there, cracked in its roots, leaning at a crazy angle, its top awry. Everywhere were splintered and fallen trees. The brush was flattened and rivulets of water ran back, toward the sound, which was now miraculously some 100 yards away down a sloping bank.

Hutch sat with his back against the palm, eyes puffed and closed. I touched his shoulder. He opened swollen eyelids, and after a moment a faint smile tried to crack his chalky face. He nudged Ed, and Ed woke up painfully. He looked at Hutch and at me but no one spoke. Then Hutch said, "Hell, we'll be late for breakfast."

Ed tried to answer but failed. Then he tried to grin but that failed too.

My knees would barely support me. They were flimsy, yet so stiff they felt as if they belonged to someone else. My right pants leg was gone and among the smaller cuts an ugly gash puckered at me from the calf. Hutch seemed unhurt beyond a twisted knee, but Ed, stripped naked, was a mass of small cuts and bright greening bruises that made an awful background for ridges of clotted blood. He said suddenly: "I've got to get to Lucy."

"We're on the west shore," Hutch answered indirectly. "Better start headin' west; there's a railroad runs a mile or so in."

We staggered behind Hutch for an hour until we found a set of rusty rails and Hutch said, "We'll go south. That's toward home, anyway."

Two agonized hours later we came to Kenny, a little station 10 miles north of West Palm Beach. The agent put us into his car, and when I woke up I was home, and my house was, unharmed. The phone lines were down so my wife drove Ed home. She was back before I got to sleep, reporting Ed—rapidly recovering—was all mouth and a new papa. Most of the houses away from the water were safe. The hurricane had headed for the interior and Palm Beach was already clearing its debris. It was more than two weeks before I heard from Hutch Newsom again. He came into the store and bought a package of shear pins and a grappling hook, and we discussed my water-ruined show window. "One thing I was right about, anyway," Hutch said sheepishly.

"What's that?" I asked, suspiciously. My leg still hurt.

"I said we'd get that car back across the wash when the wind died. Well, I got it all back—today. I've got it layin' all over the back yard. Want to go marsh-hen huntin' tomorrow, when I get it put back together?"

"No thanks." I said. "I'd rather stay home and have a baby."

Outdoor Life, March 1954

Grancel Fitz's Last Trophy

by Grancel Fitz

Fitz (right) shown with professional hunter Frank Miller and craggy-horned Maswa Cape buffalo author dropped with .375 H&H Magnum.

This is the story of Grancel Fitz's last trophy, written on assignment for
Outdoor Life. *The author numbered among his trophies all 25 legal species
of North American big game—the first man to achieve this distinction—as
well as heads from South America and Asia, but had never hunted in Africa
until this time. Modestly, he originally entitled the story "Tenderfoot in
Tanganyika." Unknown to us, as well as to most others, he had suffered several
heart attacks, the first some years ago on a grizzly hunt. Characteristically,
he kept his ailment to himself and refused to let it interfere with his activi-
ties as hunter, writer, and authority on big-game scoring until his death in
May of this year.*

—The Editor (1963)

My first safari day in Africa brought me two notable experiences in one minute. After our start from Arusha, Frank Miller had headed the Land Rover west through the parched-looking Tanganyika countryside.

Close behind us followed the big lorry loaded with camp gear. A couple of hours before sunset we took a narrow road that led into much higher country, and we seemed to be traveling just under the crest of a long ridge when Frank stopped the car.

"Bring your camera and binoculars," he said. "We can get a good view from here."

A stop for local information. Note Maté in the roof hatch.

To me, that landscape was hardly remarkable. The long, forested slope below us showed a number of open glades. Some dense brush covered the nearby skyline on the uphill side of the road, and while I'd known that Frank planned to show me something special along our way, I had no idea we had reached it as I followed him up the little rise. But we'd hardly started into those screening bushes at the top when I stopped in sheer amazement. We were on the edge—and I mean the edge—of Ngorongoro, the long-extinct volcanic crater that is 12 miles from rim to rim. Only a step in front of us, the side of this colossal bowl swooped down at a dizzy angle for 2,000 feet.

With the binoculars, I could see a distant lake in the comparatively level bottom, along with forests and open plains dotted with herds of animals. The crater is so ancient that its floor shows little sign of being volcanic. Erosion has made it ideal game country, and this was recognized years ago when the bowl and its surrounding areas were made into a sanctuary for the many species of game which drift in and out. I know that the vastness of any such spectacle can rarely be captured in a photograph, but I made a few, anyhow.

Then, in less than a minute, we walked down to the road. The four natives in back of the Land Rover were talking in Swahili. Frank pointed down the mountainside. In one of those open glades, a short way below us, I saw my first Cape buffalo. And that was another experience to be vividly remembered.

Like everyone else interested in these matters, I'd read dozens of accounts of the buffalo's vindictive thoroughness in working over his victims until there was almost nothing left, and knew he'd often been described as the most dangerous of all game. So while this one stood broadside, staring at us, I welcomed the chance to size up the kind of animal I wanted to hunt more than any other in Africa. The short-legged, stubby-faced, helmet-horned beast bulged all over with muscle, and I guessed he'd weigh a ton. At last, leaving him standing in his sanctuary like a dark statue, we went back to the car.

"What's your opinion of the buffalo as a dangerous animal?" I asked Frank as we started away.

"A man can get too reckless with any of the big five," he said, "but you can often turn a rhino, a lion, an elephant, or a leopard with a punishing shot. You can't turn a charging bull. You've got to kill him, or you've had it."

"How often do they charge before you shoot at them?"

"Very rarely," he replied. "But you can never count on it. You might meet one that some poacher has shot up."

He also explained that cows with young calves are sometimes aggressive, and that a bull may attack with no provocation after a fight with another. Sick bulls, he said, are especially unpredictable. Aside from the periodic epidemics of rinderpest, a few herds get this malady every year. An infected herd may run like any other when first alarmed. But when you follow those buffaloes into cover, knowing nothing about their illness, you are likely to be ambushed by one or two bulls and charged without warning.

On the drive to our first camping place—an overnight location—we didn't even bother to put up tents. There I began to get better acquainted with Frank Miller, at age 40 a senior professional hunter for Tanganyika Tours and Safaris, Ltd., the company in Arusha I'd chosen in booking my safari. Before my trip was half over, this Tanganyika-born Englishman proved to be one of the finest and hardest-working guides I've ever known. I believe he'd rank very close to the top among the really gifted white hunters in Africa. Particularly, on that first day, we talked about the unusual sort of hunt I had in mind.

Most men on their first safaris want general bags, with as many kinds of trophies as they can get. I didn't. I'd crowded my home in New York with North American, South American, and Asiatic heads. In 35 years of serious big-game hunting, I'd been fortunate enough to bag trophies of all 25 legal species of North American big game. With no room left to hang more than a couple of African specimens, I hoped to shoot only a trophy buffalo and—on the outside chance that we might be lucky enough to see one—an exceptionally fine lion. So I hadn't bought supplementary licenses for elephant, greater or lesser kudu, oryx, or sable antelope.

"We'll find plenty of buffaloes," Frank assured me. "I'll show you some lions, too. Trouble is that almost all the big-maned lions are in the preserves."

The following morning our lorry crew went on to pitch camp near a game-department station called Kimali. Frank and I drove to the little town of Maswa, where the district commissioner had promised him permits for both lion and buffalo in the Maswa Controlled Area. All of Kenya and much of northern Tanganyika is now divided into controlled areas similar to the "shooting blocks" of India, reserved for one safari at a time. While baiting for lion is no longer permitted in any of them, there was some possibility we might see a good one on our buffalo hunt. The Maswa region borders the west side of the famous Serengeti preserve, which contains some of the finest lions in the world.

We were given the buffalo permit at once. When the D. C. found no lion permits in his quota, he wired a request for one to the head game ranger of the district, but as this official might be away in the field, we had no assurance of a prompt answer.

"He'll send it to Kimali when it comes through," Frank said as we drove to camp. "The country south of there is uncontrolled, so we can put out some lion baits while we're waiting. We just might be lucky."

As things turned out, more than a week passed before we learned that our Maswa lion permit was unobtainable. The area had been recently closed for lion, so we didn't get back to the Maswa region for 16 days.

But what an eventful interlude that was!

We saw more than 20 different species of game in widely varying terrain, and I could have collected heads of practically all of them. Shooting only to get lion baits and camp meat for ourselves and the 10 natives in our outfit, I clobbered zebras, wildebeeste, and warthogs, along with a Thomson's gazelle, an eland, a reedbuck, and a hartebeeste.

Oddly, the four zebras the law allows gave me the most trouble. When we didn't want one, lots of them were usually standing around at close range. If we needed a lion bait in a hurry, though, we had to drive all over the country to find zebras, and they were wild as hawks. In scrubby brush country, they soon proved I wasn't so hot on 250-yard running shots; I missed more often than I connected.

While this region had no buffaloes, it had a few rhinos, which are now protected completely in Tanganyika. One gave us a tense minute when he chased the Land Rover across rock-studded ground; Frank had to do some fancy driving to get away. Also, on eight different days, we found elephants without looking for them. A hunter after a general bag would have been happy with the biggest bull we saw. His tusks would have weighed about 60 pounds each, and as he never knew we were there, we could hardly have failed to get a shot at him after a short stalk.

On another day, we were following a trail across a heavily forested hillside when Frank suddenly stopped. He was far more excited than I'd ever seen him.

"Up there is a greater kudu with fantastic horns," he said. "Fantastic."

In a small opening in the cover, not over 200 yards up the hill, I saw two kudu bulls together. Frank hadn't bothered to mention one with a fair head, and I understood why as soon as I turned my binoculars on his companion. This giant stood facing us, not even twitching his big ears, with nothing to obstruct our view of him.

How good was he? I had carefully studied a beautiful head with 58-inch horns in the Tanganyika Tours and Safaris office in Arusha, and this one was bigger in every way. His wide-flaring horns may not have been many inches longer (their more open spirals made them hard for me to judge), but they were much heavier, and when Frank said they had a 40-inch spread, I couldn't doubt it.

For a full two minutes the gorgeous bull faced us, his broad chest offering a perfect mark for a scope-sighted rifle. Then, as if he under-stood perfectly that I had no kudu license, he turned broadside and watched us for two or three minutes more. With him in that position, the shot would have been a cinch. I had always thought of a greater-kudu head as one of the world's handsomest trophies, but even when I had wall space left to hang one, I'd never dreamed of a specimen as fine as this. It was maddening.

"If we could have a bit of luck like that with a lion..." Frank began, and left the sentence unfinished. He turned away, shaking his head.

This started a new train of thought. I was a raw tenderfoot in Africa. Many times I studied clear footprints without being able to identify the animals that made them. To make things worse, I had only some book knowledge of the local game species, and the strange shapes and colors of those beasts in the unfamiliar cover made them hard for me to see. But I was beginning to understand how a present-day East African safari compares with hunts on other continents.

While everyone now knows that the amount of game left in Africa is a fast-dwindllng fraction of what it was a generation ago, the quantity we saw surprised me. I couldn't think of another country where you can run across a dozen kinds of shootable animals in a single day, as we did occasionally. It is also still possible to get some trophies of superb quality, like the kudu we'd just met and a fabulous roan antelope I saw later, and I knew about the successful safari Frank had taken out just before mine. His client, Jim Codding of California, had bagged a huge leopard, as well as one of the best sable antelope ever shot in Tanganyika, with massive horns more than 45 inches long. And that was on an 18-day, general-bag hunt.

Furthermore, even old-timers concede that a few kinds of game are as plentiful as ever. We saw impala constantly. I never tired of watching their grasshopper leaps when they were alarmed. Elephants are so destructive that government hunters must take out about 4,000 a year, and many white residents make their own annual hunts for ivory, just as an Alaska settler hunts his moose for winter meat. Right now elephants in Tanganyika are both numerous and increasing.

On the other hand, lions have taken a beating, as I learned almost as soon as I landed in Africa. They used to be considered pests and shot on sight, regardless of age or sex. Sometimes this view was undoubtedly justified. Forty years ago, when man-eaters were common in the Tabora region, Frank Miller's father killed more than 200 lions in 30 months, hunting at night with a motor bike and an acetylene lamp. More recently, I believe that lions are the only African species which has been seriously reduced by sport shooting. The others, particularly rhinos, have suffered mainly through native poaching and the settlement of new land, and many thousands of hoofed animals were needlessly slaughtered in programs for tsetse-fly control, which didn't work. But safari outfitting grew into really big business after World War II, and every visiting sportsman wanted to shoot a lion.

Today, only great luck can turn up a big-maned specimen where they aren't protected. It is much like hoping to see a record-class whitetail deer where the hunting pressure limits a buck's life expectancy to less than three years. About the only time to bag an old male is when he has temporarily strayed out of a preserve, for in areas where lions can be baited, they have almost no chance of living long enough to grow manes of trophy quality. Females, fortunately, are now illegal game. So while Frank's best efforts brought 11 lions to our baits, I wasn't surprised none tempted me.

"How long has it been since a man could be fairly sure of finding one with a full mane growing back to his shoulders, in maybe a month of hunting?" I once asked.

"They weren't too scarce right after the war," Frank said. "The war years gave them a rest. But those old lions didn't last long after that."

Some other aspects showed me how times have changed. The greatest change is in the speed, ease, and comfort with which a safari can be made.

With a minimum of red tape, I'd handed my rifles to a shipping agent at home, and found them waiting for me in Arusha, where my shooting licenses were bought. Instead of making the long and more expensive sea voyage of the old days, I had traveled on sumptuous Alitalia jet planes which took me from New York to Rome in less than eight hours, and then—after I'd enjoyed a few days in Italy—on down to Nairobi in an incredible 5½ hours. There is also fast air service between Nairobi and Arusha, but I preferred seeing Africa by bus.

Other things impressed me after the hunting began. The luxury of standard African outfitting is too well known to need description, but I'd been wondering about the attitude of the natives. In Tanganyika I found no slightest sign of trouble. Our crew couldn't have been more pleasant, and their smooth efficiency, in everything from pitching camp to preparing trophies, had come from long and careful training.

Only the weather caused us any concern. A severe drought that had afflicted much of East Africa for nearly three years was broken by unprecedented rains. In Kenya, where the Tana River overflowed its banks for as much as 30 miles, decent hunting for some safaris was literally washed out. While we didn't have many showers where we were, we could see them falling in the Maswa country north of us, and Frank postponed our buffalo hunt there for about a week. He wanted to give that area a chance to dry out, for the soil can bog down any motorized transport when it gets wet. When we did go, we left our heavy lorry behind, to avoid getting stuck, but there was one incident before we quit the country below Kimali that deserves mention.

As I'd shot leopards in India, I wanted no more of those, though there seemed to be many around. We saw five while driving to camp after dark, and ran across another in the daytime. Then one evening when we were heading back through brushy country, a black leopard crossed the trail in front of us. Seeing it clearly in the beams of the headlights, Frank and I were astonished. This color phase is said to be common in parts of Ethiopia, but it's the greatest of rarities elsewhere in Africa. That "black panther" might have made a unique trophy under different circumstances, but all shooting is illegal in East Africa between sunset and sunrise.

At last came the sunny morning when Frank thought the Maswa could be safely invaded. If we found it dry enough, he planned to get the lorry in later, but we started with the usual four helpers in the back of the Land Rover and a sketchy but adequate outfit. The indispensable native was Maté, a hard-bitten, middle-aged gunbearer of the M'tende tribe, who is also an excellent tracker.

"We'll stop in at Gavin Anderson's diamond camp," Frank said. "Those boys can tell us how things are."

I knew that a lot of prospecting is being done by Williamson Diamonds, Ltd., owned jointly by DeBeers and the Tanganyika Government.

Heading into the controlled area on one of the diamond company's new roads, we had driven for not more than an hour when Maté stopped us by slapping the top of the car. As usual, that eagle-eyed character had been standing with his head out of the roof hatch, and he'd spotted some buffaloes among the scrubby trees to our left. They were several hundred yards away. The noise of our approach hadn't bothered them; doubtless they were used to hearing the Williamson trucks. So we slipped out to see what kinds of heads they carried.

The wind was in our faces as we walked into the thin forest, and soon we found ourselves dealing with an uncommonly big herd. Along with those in front of us, there were others as far to both sides as the trees would let us see, so we had to avoid passing some that might get our scent. I understood that a bull with a 40-inch spread was considered a trophy specimen. A spread of 45 inches or better is a prize. I saw several that looked at least that big, though the cover made it hard to judge.

"Look at the spread on that one," I whispered.

"Cow," Frank replied as we silently moved on.

A moment later I spotted an unmistakable bull with another wide-spreading head. But again Frank vetoed it.

"Too young. Horn bosses are narrow, and they don't come close to meeting in the center," he explained, and he pointed to a much heavier buffalo that had just appeared. "Now, there is a heavy-headed old one, but his horns are short. The tips are worn off too much."

This was the kind of hunting I thoroughly enjoyed. There seemed every reason to hold out for an especially fine trophy, with so many to choose from, and I was getting a quick education in what a buffalo head should be. Following me like a shadow, Maté carried my .375 Magnum, a Model 70 Winchester. This is the lightest caliber now legal for dangerous East African game. Frank carried his own .458, a caliber he highly recommends, and he managed the stalking so well that we inspected several other promising bulls in the next hour.

The big-bodied, old bulls with the wide, thick horn bosses impressed me most. It seemed logical that one of those would represent a better trophy, and taking them would surely be better conservation than shooting the younger herd bulls, no matter what spreads they carried. The problem was to find a massive-headed old bull with long enough horns and good conformation.

In the end, of course, we alarmed them to the point where we couldn't hope to get close again without giving them a long rest. The scattered bands had joined up when we saw them last, and as they streamed out of the scrub into an open place half a mile away, we learned that there were at least 250 animals in the herd.

Turning back toward the car, I reflected that the scoring system for buffaloes used by the Conseil International de la Chasse makes a lot more sense than the British method of ranking them by spread alone. It gives an old bull the credit he deserves by measuring the massiveness of each horn at three places, to offset the length he has worn away. Some cows and young bulls showed wider spreads and longer horns than any I'd seen in that whole bunch, and this, Frank told me, was very often so.

We drove on to the diamond camp, and there we stopped for a chat.

When the prospectors reported more buffaloes a dozen miles farther up the road, we kept right on going. The scrub-covered terrain gave way to open plains, and on them we saw topi and bands of Grant's gazelles as well as Thomson's gazelles and many hartebeeste.

Early that afternoon, when the road topped a little rise, we saw buffaloes scattered out to the left of us a quarter of a mile away. There were about 150. To my surprise—for they couldn't scent us—they promptly took off on a course that brought them gradually closer to the road ahead. I soon learned that their gait, a rocking, lumbering kind of gallop, was a lot faster than it looked. Our speedometer showed about 25 miles an hour, and the whole herd was keeping up with us. We slowed down, looking for big heads. In another minute they were crossing the road, and as we watched the parade go by, a bull toward the rear struck me as a stand-out.

"I'll never try to outrun one of those beasts," I said as they raced away. "The whole bunch was going faster than any human sprinter ever ran on an Olympic track."

"They can keep it up for miles, too," Frank told me. "I've seen them run to the tops of high, steep-sided ridges without slowing down. We'll let them alone for an hour; then we'll try to sneak up on that wide-horned bull."

The buffaloes kept going until they reached a big patch of cover nearly a mile away, but they slackened their pace as they entered. We stayed put. After finishing lunch, we drove off in a new direction, making the stalk against the wind when we left the car.

Half an hour later, the bull I'd wanted to see again stood calmly looking at me, hardly 65 yards from us. The spread of his horns must have been 48 inches, maybe 50, and they curved out and turned inward in beautiful conformation. But there was a five-inch gap between the rather narrow bases of his horns, and the Cape buffalo heads I like best have those wide, rugged-looking bosses that almost jam against each other. That is one feature which sets them apart from all other buffaloes in the world. I turned to Frank with an unspoken question. He shook his head. Then the usually silent Maté ended my temptation with a single comment.

"Bura," he said in Swahili. "Nothing."

We quietly retreated to the car and turned toward the road, but we soon saw something that stopped us. Off across a narrow plain to the north was a half-a-mile strip of low, sparse brush alive with traveling game. A seemingly endless column of wildbeeste, zebras, and kongoni kept coming out of heavier growth to the northwest and moving through the strip to where all these animals disappeared into some fairly dense cover to the east. While I gave up trying to count them, we surely saw 1,000 in the minutes we watched.

"They've been over near Lake Victoria since the drought burned up the feed in the Serengeti preserve," Frank said. "Now that the rains have started, they're going back."

In the rest of the afternoon we saw no other notable heads, though we found some small bunches of buffaloes, which brought our count to more than 500 of them since we'd entered the Maswa area that morning. But we also ran into difficult traveling after a drenching rain. At two places on the road, the Land Rover sank so far into the mud we had to use a winch to haul out. When we finally turned back toward camp, we were barely able to cross a little brook with steep, high banks that had turned slippery. The place had given us no trouble on the earlier crossing, and there was no reason to suspect the part this brook would play before our hunt was over.

Gavin Anderson and his men had invited us to stay at the diamond camp. We spent a most interesting evening there, and that night I went to bed thinking that the day had been as memorable as any I'd ever spent in game country, though I hadn't fired a shot. We had seen more than 1,500 animals. The figure might easily have been doubled if we'd watched that migrating horde a little longer. With so many buffaloes in the area, I felt sure I'd soon have an outstanding trophy.

At dawn we drove out to locate the first big herd of the day before. It had rained hard again in the night, washing out a lot of tracks. The lower parts of the country off the road were too soft to cross, so we decided to let them dry out for a few hours in the hot sun. Having seen nothing unusual except the first cheetah of the trip—the 26th kind of large animal I'd noted since our hunt began—we headed north again for the open plains.

We spotted less game than usual on the way. When we came to the brook with the high, sloping banks, my hopes of finding a trophy bull that morning dropped considerably. The little stream had become an uncrossable torrent.

"One of Gavin's lads mentioned a higher trail east of here," Frank said. "We might walk that way for a bit and see the lay of the land."

When Maté loaded our rifles, the three of us scrambled up the little slope to the right of the road.

Directly ahead we saw a fairly sizable expanse in which the low, thorny silale trees reminded me of a long-abandoned orchard. The underbrush was mainly "singing thorn," named for the noise a high wind makes when it blows through them. Perhaps 1½ miles away, this growth ended in a small plain. But the visibility in the nearby cover wasn't bad, and after we'd gone only 200 yards we began to find more game than we'd seen in all that bright, sunny morning. Many kongoni were there, along with a few warthogs, zebras, roans, elands, wildebeestes, and ostriches. Before long we added steinboks, dikdiks, Tommies, and Grant's gazelles to this list.

We also saw something else that wasn't nearly so welcome. Off to the northeast, some dark clouds were dropping a curtain of rain. Worse yet, a bigger storm had started between us and the diamond camp, roughly 15 miles from where we stood. Frank began to look worried.

"I'm afraid we'll have to leave the Maswa this afternoon," he said. "With the road no worse than it is now, our lorry couldn't possibly come in. And if we have more of these storms, we might not get the Land Rover out for a month."

We'd gone about a mile from the car when Maté spotted buffaloes. They were fairly close, on the windward side of a trail we'd been following. We hadn't been discovered. The herd was moving slowly; we could see little except some dark patches shifting among the trees. We'd commented on how quickly the whole region turned green after the rains had come, but I hadn't realized how many new leaves had sprouted until I tried to pick out a bull.

Here was a real problem. More than any other animals I can think of, buffaloes rely almost equally on eyes, ears, and nose, and all those senses seem excellent. We didn't know the number in this herd. Along with the risk of stampeding them all by spooking an unseen one, we had to think about the other game, for even a startled dikdik could spoil the whole show.

As the herd worked through half a mile of cover to the edge of the plain, we learned there were 30 to 40 buffaloes in it. The biggest was an old, huge-bodied bull, but we hadn't been able to tell much about his head except that the bosses seemed very wide. Then I saw them all start out into the open. I'd taken my rifle from Maté, and when we made a hurried approach to the last screen of thornbush, I had my first clear sight of the bull's massive, helmetlike horns. He was well under 100 yards away.

"The spread is nothing to brag about," Frank whispered. "It's around 40. The bosses are fine."

"Hang the spread. He has character," I answered, trying to slip into a more open place to shoot without scaring him. But I must have botched that job; I moved, and the whole herd bolted.

The bull was angling toward my left when I shot first, the bullet hitting ahead of that flank as I aimed to drive it through to his far shoulder. It didn't stop him, but he slowed so much that I missed in front of him when he turned almost broadside, and the next shot wasn't so accurate, either. I tried for the spine, about 14 inches below his withers. Instead of connecting there, I tagged the center of his shoulder. And that 300-grain Silvertip bullet killed him, not 20 yards from where he'd been when my first shot was fired.

When we walked over and examined the old bull's head, even Maté was jubilant about it. The massive, rough-hewn bosses were as wide and closely set as I'd thought, and the deep dips of the symmetrical horns gave them good length for a trophy of that age and compact type.

So, while admirers of extreme spreads may think I made a tenderfoot's choice, I liked this buffalo better than any other we'd seen— and better than any we found in the Lolkisale region a week later, when we were far away from the threat of Maswa mud. Maybe his picture shows why I was so contented with him.

Outdoor Life, September 1963

Fred Bear at 80

BY CLARE
CONLEY

The Man Who Made Modern Bowhunting Possible

In the early 1940s a seemingly
insignificant event took place. A
man from New York, who worked
for the Corning Glass Company, walked
into a small archery company in Detroit,
Michigan.

In his hand he had a piece of fabric woven from tiny fibers of glass.
It was a novelty—cloth made of glass—and the owner of the company saw it that way until the New York man mentioned that glass in
this form was slightly elastic. It would stretch about 3 percent.

That remark combined instantly with another piece of knowledge that the bow maker had in his mental catalog of information. And this was the moment the birth of modern archery and bowhunting took place. That unknown bow maker had two pieces of information and the common sense to combine them. This was the cornerstone of the $150 million-a-year business archery is today.

That bow maker was Fred Bear. And what he also knew was that a glue recently had been invented by Chrysler Corporation that would hold rubber to metal under extreme conditions. That glue, called 5509, was the first epoxy.

Bear wondered. Could 5509 be combined with glass cloth to create a new material that could be bonded to the front and back of bows making them stronger, lighter and certainly more durable than the yew, hickory and osage wood bows dominant at that time? The chief chemist of Chrysler, Don Swazey, agreed to saturate several layers of the cloth with the epoxy, then put it in a press and cure it at 325°.

Bear found that the new fiberglass and epoxy material worked well on the outside, or back, of bows, but not on the inside, or belly. The woven glass on the inside kinked and crushed under the compression. A different material would have to be used on the inside—aluminum. With more help from Chrysler, Bear was able to make the first bow using fiberglass. It had a fiberglass back and aluminum belly.

But unlike other bows of the time, its limbs were wide and flat like a leaf from a car spring. Also, the limbs were light and would spring forward quickly.

"The first one I made I covered with masking tape so no one could see how it was built. And when archers would come into the office I would hand it to them and ask them what they thought of it," recalls Bear.

"The bow looked like it might pull twenty pounds. The archers were amazed at how strong the bow was for its size. Then when they shot it they were more amazed at the arrow speed. Later developments didn't do a whole lot more than that. That first bow was the breakthrough with glass."

Soon after that, Bear developed a way of making glass in which strands only ran lengthwise on the bow limb. Fiberglass could then be used on the inside of the limbs as well as the outside. Bow making has virtually stayed the same since.

For the first time a person could walk into a sporting-goods store and buy the best bow that could be built right off the shelf. Fiberglass made possible the mass production of bows. The lone artisan in his shop shaving out a single bow at a time from a stave of wood was a thing of the past.

Fred Bear in one step had advanced bow design from the long bow that the English took on the Crusades in the 10th and 11th centuries up to the 20th century. Actually, laminated bows with recurving limbs were an ancient Turkish design. Sinew was used on the outside and horn on the inside, but no waterproof adhesive was known, and when the bows got wet they came apart. Bear had eliminated the weight and slowness of the English bow and the structural defects of the Turkish design.

Fred Bear was born the son of a toolmaker in Carlisle, Pennsylvania, on March 5, 1902. From his father, who lived to be 85, he acquired a love of working with tools and building things. From his rural surroundings he gained a love of the outdoors, and in particular, a love of horses.

The first joint of the third finger of Fred Bear's right hand is missing as a permanent reminder of that farm life. His sister cut it off with a hand-operated hay chopper. Young Fred and his sister were cutting hay to prepare a mixture of horse feed. The first step required chopping the hay into short lengths in a trough-like cutter with a shear handle, like a paper cutter.

Fred fed the hay and his sister chopped. Soon it developed into a game. Fred would put the hay in and pull it back before his sister could cut it. With a little experience she began to plan ahead, and Fred's hand didn't quite clear the chopper.

Fred rushed to the house where his two Mennonite aunts treated the remainder of the finger with lily leaves and rosewater while they took the time to clean the boy up before going to see the doctor. Even the tips of his socks, which were sticking out of holes in his shoes, were summarily snipped off with scissors.

Bear in later years became a left-handed archer, which meant he could draw the bowstring with his left hand. This may be a result of his childhood accident, because he shoots both a rifle and shotgun right-handed.

In his late 20s Fred Bear moved to Detroit where he worked in a company that subcontracted work from the major car companies. Bear worked up to managing the operations—but a problem soon became apparent. The Great Depression was on and the owner of the company needed cash. Twice he tried to set the place on fire, but each time Fred discovered it in time. The third time, he didn't.

Out of work and with no jobs around, Fred teamed up with a man who had connections that could get them subcontracting work from Chrysler. In 1933 these two men, with a total of $1,200 in tools and cash, opened up shop in a large garage. They did silk-screen work for the car companies on such things as tire covers. But in one corner of the building, Bear started another tiny venture. It couldn't pay its own way, but Fred wanted it. The company was called Bear Archery.

Fred knew how to make bows but he soon realized he would have to create a market for them. First came the Detroit Archery Club, but Fred noticed another possibility.

"I found that the newspapers would run the scores from archery tournaments we had but it didn't mean anything. However, if you gave them a picture of a deer or a bear that some archer shot, that might make the front page. So I got in the promotion business."

Bear has been promoting archery and bowhunting ever since.

By 1939 both companies had grown and the partners split it up. Bear took the archery company and continued with it in Detroit through World War II. But he wanted to move out of town, so Bear Archery was incorporated with three stock holders. His original partner sold his business and bought stock, a friend put in $20,000, and Bear's holdings, the majority, were the remainder making the total about $100,000. In 1947 they moved the company to Grayling, Michigan. Calamity was waiting for them there.

The small corporation was short of money. Just at the moment when it needed to do some business and make money, an all-aluminum bow came on the market. For a year, until problems in it began to show up, the aluminum bow captured the market and nearly broke Bear Archery. For two years during the warm months, Fred Bear and his wife lived in a tent along the Manastee River to keep costs down.

Though the fiberglass laminated bow was a revolutionary break-through, it still hadn't taken a major share of the small bow market. But by 1950-51, Bear had worked out a way to make uni-directional glass that eliminated the cross threads, so the material could be used on the inside of the bow as well. Fiberglass bows were on their way. Nothing would ever stop them.

In 1960 a mysterious increase in bow breakage occurred, and put the company on the ropes again. Bear was determined to replace every bow that broke and about one out of five did. The reason, which took two years to discover, was in the face of two of the heated presses in which bows were made. The face had warped and would not properly bond the laminations.

Another problem was winters in Grayling. The very dry winter air in northern Michigan caused the wood in the bows to dry out. Bows made in winter and later used in humid climates absorbed moisture in the wood and broke the laminations.

In 1960-61 Bear Archery was in serious trouble. It had lost $180,000 through breakage. The company was making television cabinets for Admiral for extra income, but they still owed the IRS about $15,000.

"The IRS came to Grayling and picked up a state policeman. They were going to lock the place up."

Fred was out in the plant when his financial man came out with the news. "It looks like we've had it. The IRS is here and we haven't any money in the bank. What are we going to do?"

And Bear replied, "Well, I'm just going to keep on working, and you're going back in there and sell them some kind of a bill of goods."

What he did was give the IRS a bad check for $500 and convinced them to take it. When the check returned, the Grayling bank was supposed to warn Fred, but this time they missed. The check was bounced. But Bear had friends who believed in him. He explained the desperate situation to one of them and ended by saying he needed $500 for 30 days. The man turned to his wife and asked her for his checkbook.

People seemed to want to help Fred Bear. One of his employees, a bachelor, realized things were tough for the company. He took his paychecks, but refused to cash them for six to eight months.

For another 10 years of amazing growth, Bear Archery continued as an independent company. But offers to buy were frequent and attractive. Finally the corporation sold to Victor, and Victor a few years later was taken over by Kidde, the present parent company of Bear Archery. Also, in the late 1970s the company moved to Gainesville, Florida.

Fred Bear is one of the few people alive today who was a personal friend of Art Young—the Young of Pope and Young, the recognized trophy-record keeping organizaton of bowhunting. In fact, Bear's first interest in the sport came from seeing Art Young put on a demonstration of shooting at a Rotary Club in Detroit. Young made his living putting on such shows, although he had gained fame through films on bowhunting in Africa and Alaska. Bear did not know Dr. Saxton Pope, a medical professor at the University of California who teamed up with Young on several hunts. Young was 10 years older than Bear, but he died when he was 45 of a ruptured appendix.

"He was my hero. Anything he said was gospel," Fred remembers. "He was a great, clean-living fellow. Big guy, good looking, no bad habits. I was kind of amazed I could keep up with this guy in roving." (A type of shooting in which archers roam, picking targets and seeing who can come the closest.) Young never shot in tournaments.

"At that time archers had different ways of measuring how good they were. One was to see how many arrows they could keep in the air at a time. Young used a Mongolian release that lends itself to fast shooting because it combines nocking the arrow and pulling the string. He could shoot fast."

However, few people know that Fred Bear about this time was the Michigan State Target Champion.

Fred Bear in his own way became a much greater advocate of bowhunting than either Pope or Young ever dreamed of. For one thing, by the time Bear began to make promotional films of his adventures and to appear on television on "The American Sportsman" and "Arthur Godfrey" shows, bows of quality were readily available to anyone who wanted to try the sport. So there was much more potential to bring people into bowhunting. Bear also made many more films and through television reached millions more people.

Bear's hunting trips to India, Africa, South America, Alaska and the Arctic had as their reason the promotion of bowhunting and Bear Archery. But Fred loves to hunt, too. At one time, Bear held five Pope and Young trophy records. He still holds two, brown bear and stone sheep.

Although the first big game he bagged with a bow was a deer in northern Michigan in 1935, Fred Bear's favorite animal to hunt is—naturally—bear. Once on a hunt in British Columbia he saw 62 grizzlies in 25 days. Some of his tightest moments have also come on bear hunts.

On a grizzly hunt to make a television film for ABC, he was charged by a sow grizzly that put him up a tree and kept him there from late one afternoon to 8:30 a.m. the next day.

He was charged by polar bears twice. The second charge came instantly after Fred had hit it with an arrow at 30 yards. At 20 yards the guide dropped the bear with a rifle. Fred walked over to it to pull out his arrow. At that moment the bear stood up, and Fred had to kill it with a .44 Magnum handgun. The rifle shot had only creased the bear's head, stunning it.

In Africa, Bear along with his white hunter and natives were pinned in a small brush blind for half a night by a lion that could have jumped in on them at any second.

But sometimes his hunts resulted in amazing twists. When I was hunting with him in Alaska he shot a bull moose at 15 feet. And then there was his Indian tiger.

Perched in the top of a palm tree, Fred was waiting for the beaters to drive the tiger past. This was in a small canyon. Suddenly Bear saw the cat about 90 or 100 yards away. It was pacing back and forth at the base of the rimrock that formed the side of the canyon. It was apparently trying to find a way to go over the side.

"Finally I decided that maybe if I shot an arrow beyond the tiger, he might turn back my way. So I picked my poorest arrow and shot it. I hit the tiger right through the lungs and killed him."

Innovating, designing, promoting, hunting, Fred Bear has led the way. During the interviews for this article, I tried to encourage Fred Bear to describe his role in the development of American bowhunting particularly in relation to Pope and Young. Politely, he dodged the question.

It took a while, but eventually I figured why. Without Fred Bear, there is a chance that the modern fiberglass laminated bow would either not have been invented or would have been invented much later. Without Fred Bear but even with the fiberglass laminated bow, the promotion of bowhunting might never have taken place.

So what does it all boil down to? Well for one thing, without Fred Bear there probably wouldn't have been a Pope and Young Club. Think about it. Bear made the sport that created the organization. I'll bet that Saxton Pope and Art Young would welcome having a name like Fred Bear alongside theirs. Pope, Young and Bear. And at 80 years old, the only one left to enjoy the honor.

Outdoor Life, March 1982

A Lost Soul

BY DAN DE FOE

"A covered wagon, drawn by a span of large but bony horses."

The Marie du Chien Valley is one of the most fruitful and enchanting in the southwest part of Missouri, and Jethro Cushman owned one of the most fruitful and enchanting plantations to be found within its limits.

Brother Cushman was a Presbyterian of the old school, one who insisted, always, that his children should obey his behests, even as he tried to obey those of the Almighty. His pride and the pride of his family was the youngest daughter, Marie, a tall, handsome girl of sixteen, precociously developed, whose brown hair, blue eyes and sprightly mien were known and admired by scores of the young gentry of the region.

It is sad, but true, that self-willed fathers frequently find themselves confronted with problems offered by the incorrigible caprices of self-willed girls, and that was precisely the predicament in which Mr. Jethro Cushman found himself in attempting to outline and to prescribe proper paths of conduct for the 16-year-old baby. He very much desired that Marie should be a Presbyterian; she preferred to be an Episcopalian, and when the father objected to this she at once decided that she would be nothing, and thereafter strenuously adhered to the determination. The old gentleman's ideal girl was one who was demure, retiring and quiet, and he indiscreetly insisted upon the adoption of such a demeanor by a girl to whom such a task was simply a physical impossibility. As a consequence, in her determination to be natural, the daughter went to the other extreme, with the result that she was hoydenish, capricious, and a tomboy. Being, however, a young person of good impulses and warm affections it is likely that her intense pride and her devotion to an indulgent mother would have restrained her from anything more rash than occasional outbursts of temper, to be followed by reluctant obedience to her father's wishes, but for a blind and unreasoning love affair in which she became involved, and which the father determined, by an arbitrary assumption of parental authority, to crush and obliterate, entirely regardless of consequences.

It is but justice to Brother Cushman to admit that, though he had definite matrimonial ambitions with regard to his daughter, they never were declared. She was only made to understand that she ought to look for her company among the people of her father's church, and that chief among the qualifications most desirable in lover and prospective husband were respectability and wealth. In the abstract the advice could hardly have been better, but the girl shrewdly believed, and it was true, although the father had never ventured an open statement of the fact, that he would have been glad if she had encouraged the attentions of a very worthy and very wealthy young neighbor, of mediocre abilities but excellent prospects, who was educating himself for, and was expected to make his mark in, the ministry. But, as generally happens in such cases, even if the young lady had not been (which she declared in her heart of hearts that she was) madly, hopelessly, irreclaimably in love with handsome Clarence Woodruff, she decided, off-hand, that the young minister was positively the last man on her entire list of acquaintances that she would select for a husband. What encouragement has a father to do the best he can for a daughter in such a behalf?

Clarence Woodruff was not wealthy, hardly well-to-do. Worse than that, he was inclined to be wild. He attended dances and horse races; and, though not a drinker or a gambler, he was worldly minded and had the force and dash and steam of youth that plunged him ahead in conformity with his own sweet will, in utter defiance of the opinions of older and wiser heads, and this, of course, placed him under the ban of Mr. Cushman's unqualified disapproval.

When the daughter was forbidden to meet or encourage, or even think of young Woodruff, she, of course, clandestinely did all three. And when the father, in his exasperation and rage, prescribed the same terms to the lover, that worthy, in a manner characteristic of him, had the hardihood to defy him to his face. The war waxed warm, with the result that while the lovers were planning an elopement Miss Marie was suddenly and secretly conveyed by her father to a denominational school at St. Louis, where she was for some weeks held prisoner, and a prisoner who could not even send or receive a letter except under the espionage of the strictest tutors, made more strict by the peremptory directions of the girl's irascible father.

The girl's resentment was natural, but it burned in her bosom with a fierceness and intensity little suspected by her devoted parent. Regardless of the consequences, and declaring to herself that she cared nothing for the future, she planned an escape, and was so successful in executing it that while detectives were systematically searching the city she was in the private car of a wealthy but lecherous railway magnate, speeding toward the city of Chicago.

Of her life there little is known, but in a reproachful letter to her father she admitted that she had adopted an abandoned life and declared that it was her intention at once to take the jewels and finery which her official admirer had lavished upon her and escape to parts unknown.

Rumors crept back to the little community in which she had lived that she had drifted to the West, to Denver, to Leadville and other mining camps; but at home she was mourned as one dead, and the hardiest gossipers did not dare utter her name in the presence of the heartbroken father or the members of the sorrowing family.

Glenwood Springs, Colorado, was a nondescript sort of health resort in 1884, but one extensively patronized for all that. Though there was not a railroad within a hundred miles, news of the miraculous cures wrought by its wonderful hot springs had gone abroad and had attracted thither the sick and afflicted, the lame and the blind, not only from neighboring regions, but from points some times located in the most distant parts of the Union.

A large portion of the "town" was composed of tents, not only used as temporary tenements but as temporary offices and places of business. Saloons, gambling houses and maisons de joie were plentiful, and there was abroad that indescribable free-and-easy atmosphere, since entirely obliterated, that marks the inception of the "boom" town of the mountains, whether it be a prospective health resort, commercial mart or mining camp.

It was on a mellow, dreamy, autumn afternoon, such as are the boast and the glory of the western slope of Colorado, because they seem especially designed by an indulgent Creator for pleasant excursions along the adjacent trout streams, or for more exciting experiences among the different species of game that abounds among the mountain parks of that favored region. A corps of surveyors were chaining and driving stakes down in the center of the principal streets; real estate dealers were hurrying here and there disposing of choice lots to newcomers who were anxious to buy; a crowd of loafers were enjoying themselves trying the courage of a formidable looking bulldog by attempting to lead him within reach of the chains of a pair of full-grown mountain lions, the pets of a gambler at the Senate saloon. Men and women, in vehicles and on foot, with crutches and without, were passing and repassing on their way to and from the mammoth hot springs or the natural steam cave in the side of the hill above the town, as their predilections and preferences happened to lead them. Crowds poured in and out of the saloons and gambling places; and among them were women from "on the hill"—privileged in every new-born mountain town, at first, to drink and smoke and joke and swagger, the same as other loafers, and afterward, by advancing civilization, forced to retire from view and confine their operations to the houses that they occupy.

On this September morning the loafers on "Grand avenue," principally an avenue of tents, saw, entering the town from the Roaring Fork Valley, on the south, a covered wagon. It attracted attention because it was a dusty and worn-looking veteran, drawn by a span of large but bony horses, whose jaded, discouraged look told plainly that their lack of flesh was due to days of weary toiling over sandy plains and precipitous mountain passes.

When the vehicle had stopped in front of a large tent that displayed upon its flaring front the badly painted sign, "Groceries and Provisions," the clusters of loiterers saw that it contained a young man of 30, or thereabout, who occupied the spring seat in company with a woman of 25 years, presumably his wife. Two flaxen-haired girls of tender years sat upon a bundle behind the seat, while upon a bed made down in the middle of the wagon lay a woman of 50, whose thin hands, contracted joints, pale face and heavy eyes bore unmistakable evidence of the ravaging waste of disease and suffering. The driver himself, but for travel stain and a stubby growth of beard, was a man whose face and manner would have been a favorable introduction among honest men anywhere. He was large, quick spoken and with a mien that was neither bold nor shy. As he stopped he spoke confidently and respectfully to Doc McCabe, as the first man whose attention he attracted, a man, by the way, well known to many of the earlier settlers in the Grand Valley.

"Are you acquainted here?" he asked.

"Yes; as well as anybody, I guess."

"Well, stranger, I'm about broke, and —"

"Haven't got any the best o' me," answered Doc, with a careless chuckle.

"What I was goin' to say is, I've got a sick mother here, that I've hauled all the way from Bates County, Missouri. Bad luck on the road has run us short of money and I want to get into a house, the first thing, an' some teamin' or some kind of work to do right away afterward. What do you think's the show?"

"You won't be able to get a house, that's sure, thout you build it. You can get all the work you want—more, too."

"No house, eh?"

"Not a house."

"That'll be bad."

"I dunno; what's the matter with your mother? Consumption?"

"No. The doctors can't tell us. It's the drawin' up of the joints an' a wastin' away of the muscles. I brought her here because an old friend of ours by the name of Porter—lives in El Paso now—he had the same thing and these springs cured him, sound and well. Guess they're all right, ain't they?"

"I guess they are. If there's anything they won't cure we ain't found it out yet. I came here a year ago so full of sores that they wouldn't let me stay in a boarding house in this town—nor even at a hospital. I had to take blankets and sleep under those cedars over there on the side of the hill. I've taken the baths all the time since, and today I'm as healthy as anybody, am a deputy sheriff and doin' the most of the work of the office. Tell you what you do."

"I'm sure I'll be much obliged," said the stranger.

"You rig up a camp with your wagon sheet some place handy to the springs, so you can get your mother to 'em—'tain't gon' to be anything but nice weather like this till about Christmas, it always is— give your mother the baths once a day to start with and go on with your teamin', there's plenty of it to be done. You'll be all right there until you can get a house. Everybody is buildin' houses to rent and in a month there'll be houses to spare."

The stranger thanked him, gave the lines to his wife, inquired as to the present needs of their commissary and went into the tent store to make some unimportant purchases.

Hardly had he disappeared when McCabe, a master in veterinary matters, said to the wife:

"Madam, your husband's got a sick horse there."

One of the animals, indeed, showed sudden but unmistakable signs of distress, and McCabe at once summoned the husband and called his attention to the fact.

The animal was taken out of the harness immediately and the usual remedies applied, but apparently to no purpose. A boy was placed upon its back with instructions to gallop it up and down the street, the incident attracting the usual crowd of people, most of whom were, as usual, ready with suggestions and advice; but despite their efforts the animal lay down and could not again be coaxed or driven to rise. Other remedies were applied but to no effect. The beast, bloated to twice its normal proportions, groaned with pain, and when it was suggested that it would be humane to kill it, and thus end its misery, the owner declared that its death would ruin him; and the wife and children, until then silent spectators of the scene, begged the husband and father, with tears, which they made no attempt to conceal, not to allow the poor animal to be put to death.

While the crowd of sympathetic citizens were looking on, admittedly nonplussed, and the owner of the suffering horse was still drenching

"The beast, bloated to twice its normal size, groaned with pain."

it with medicine, two women of the demi-monde came by, one smoking a cigarette with evident relish, the other chatting carelessly. As they drew nearer, attracted by the crowd, the taller one, with the brown hair and blue eyes, seeing the sick horse and distressed owner kneeling at its head, gasped:

"Oh, my God!"

She came near fainting, but rallied and, by the aid of the woman who was with her, succeeded in tottering into the "Palace" saloon (a pine board shanty), where she ordered a full glass of brandy, which she hastily swallowed, then begged her companion to hurry with her to her home "on the hill."

As the two passed out the tall woman, keeping her own face from view, looked again at the stranger from Missouri, then at the worn and weary occupants of the wagon. She heard a gambler among the onlookers say:

"Guess his horse is dead."

"Yes," replied his comrade, another gambler, "and it's hard luck; broke, and with a sick family. We'll have to give him a benefit."

The tall woman immediately changed her purpose. Instead of going toward the row "on the hill" she turned and walked rapidly in the direction of the bank, a one-story structure, but an institution representing millions of money. She entered, came out, walked away again, and within five minutes a bank clerk elbowed his way through the crowd to the side of the stranger from Missouri. "What is your name?" he asked.

"Clarence B. Woodruff," answered the stranger with a puzzled expression on his sun-tanned face.

"Well, Mr. Woodruff, there's $100 up at the bank, to your credit, and more if you need it. Come in and get it whenever you're ready."

"Guess you're mistaken," declared the Missourian, candidly; "I'm a stranger here; just got in."

"No; there's no mistake, I think. You were the owner of this horse, weren't you?"

"Yes sir."

"Well, you are the man. It is all straight."

"Who done it?" asked the Missourian, still doubtingly.

"A friend; and that is all that I am at liberty to tell you."

"I need the money, God knows, an' ef I kin git it, I'll secure my note with a mor'gage on the wagon an' the other horse," he said, humbly and thankfully.

"We're not to take any note, or any mortgage," said the clerk. "You can call and get the money whenever it suits you."

The clerk hurried away, again, in the direction of the bank, leaving the Missourian standing there, dazed and dumbfounded.

His countenance was a study. Plainly he was struggling between a hope for help and the vague fear of a practical joke. His face was pale and with the lump in his throat and the conflicting emotions in his breast, he looked as though called upon to say something when to say anything was an utter impossibility. He looked appealingly at his wife, but the look his helpless partner returned him offered no clue to the mystery. He looked irresolutely at the crowd of astonished spectators, at his dead horse, at his wife again then tried twice before he could utter a word.

"I'm a-goin' up to the bank," he said, "an' ef that money is fer me, hyarafter I'll b'lieve in God and angels."

The money was for him; but he had to accept it without any explanation further than that already given. He bought a tent at once, and another horse. With plenty of work, for himself and his team, the man contrived to keep the mother and the wife and children in comparative comfort, and had the satisfaction of seeing the invalid improve from the first, and finally restored to the most perfect health.

Marie Cushman (not known by that name, however) departed immediately for Salt Lake City, and the first intimation her former lover had that he had been near her or that she was the mysterious bank depositor, was when he called at that institution to replace the sum obtained. She had left a note there to be delivered to him on that occasion, not before. It read:

Do not think of repaying any part of the money, Clarence, for my whereabouts will be unknown to the bank and I shall never get it. Do not ask about me, or try to find me, or ever think of me again.

I am lost. Good-by, forever. MARIE.

Outdoor Life, January 1898

Lifetime Buck

BY ALLEN PARSONS

Its antlers prove it is the head of a deer.

The children speak of that head as "Baa-baa." Indeed, it does somewhat suggest a sheep. The farmer-taxidermist who mounted it made the nose too pointed. The head, too, was set upon the maple shield with the full length of the neck behind it, so that it stands out from the wall in surprising fashion. It might well be an okapi or an unspotted giraffe, except for its antlers. They establish its identity. It's the head of a little three-point buck deer, that couldn't have weighed over 100 pounds. As a trophy it leaves much to be desired. But to me it's precious, for it was my first, and I shot it the night before my fifteenth birthday.

The emotions aroused by your first deer, or trout, or ruffed grouse shot on the wing, are so profound, your sense of triumph so exhilarating, that you can never forget them. But, when a beardless boy, unaided and alone, has brought down a wary deer, then sir, life has given him its richest triumph.

As a youngster in boarding school, I became a victim of too-rapid growth. I put on height but no breadth, weight, or muscle. The doctor was frank and wise. He told my father, "My medicines won't do that boy a bit of good. Outdoor air and exercise are what he needs. Get him out in the woods somewhere."

The end of June found me in an old lumber camp in southern Quebec. As companion and guardian I was given the camp cook, a French-Canadian with a name I could never make out. Two syllables in it sounded like Riley, so Riley he was to me. Riley spoke English that required an interpreter; my French was no better. With pathetic persistence, we tried constantly to converse in each other's language, and eventually we learned to catch the other's drift. When Riley said something like "Eet ees necessaire *poissons* we have *pour manger demain*," I guessed he was suggesting that I catch a mess of trout for the morrow's breakfast.

The lumber camp, in the office of which we made our home, was located in a narrow valley. Down this valley flowed a crystal stream, small, and icy cold, with a succession of miniature waterfalls and pools. It was filled with brook trout. In an hour or so before breakfast I could catch ten or a dozen, their average length being only seven or eight inches. Once in a while, I would proudly show Riley a noble fish at least ten inches long, and revel in his "Magnifique!" The largest I ever took there was about eleven inches long, and his hooked lower jaw and venerable appearance told me that he was truly one of the giants of that brook.

Unlike so many of his compatriots, Riley was no spiritual brother of the coureur de bois and the voyageur. He could never be persuaded to go fishing, and deer tracks left him cold. Though in the woods, he was not of them. Even his manner of dressing bore that out. He favored white, starched collars, laundered carefully by himself, and worn with a black string tie. The clerical aspect of this strange woods garb was completed by a low-crowned, black felt hat, without which one never saw him save when he took to his bunk at bedtime. Then, when he doffed it and hung it carefully on a peg, his round poll appeared indecently nude, for Riley was bald to his ears. But, if the forest, with its fish and game, were not his passion, music was. As soon as breakfast was finished, and I was off with my little fly rod, Riley would pick up his violin. He would seat himself in the wooden armchair outside, with a sigh of pleasure for the joys to come. Back he would tilt against the wall of the cabin, hook his heels into the chair rounds, close his eyes, and ply the bow. As I worked up the stream, putting the Parmachene Belle over likely little pools, I would hear that violin until it died away in the distance.

Before I had gone north, I had, through channels of boyish barter beginning with the capital of a bicycle, acquired a .32 Stevens rifle. I have never heard this caliber of rifle well spoken of for deer hunting, but to me, it was beyond all doubt the finest rifle that money could buy. I had plenty of cartridges, and almost every afternoon practiced shooting. My target was a sheet of wrapping paper, fastened with pitch to a big maple tree. The distance was fifty paces. At first I consistently missed even the tree. When I first put a bullet into the paper, I had to summon Riley to be a witness to the achievement.

Then, with practice, I hit the paper more often until, finally, I could get all my shots into it. True, some of them might cut the edges, but the bullets were there. I practiced standing, sitting, prone, and kneeling shots, and came to know the feel and the whimsies of that rifle.

So the summer passed pleasantly, and I picked up weight and strength amazingly. While doing my target shooting, there had been no thought that I would be able to do any hunting that season, but one day, toward the first of September, there came word that the opening of school had been delayed until the second week in October. Here was an opportunity long desired. There were many deer in those woods. Their tracks were all along the brook. Occasionally at dusk as I came pussy-footing along the stream in my moccasins, I would hear the sudden crash of the brush, and see the disappearing white flag of a doe, perhaps with a fawn.

About the middle of September the trout fishing, hitherto unvaryingly good, became poor. Pools that had never failed to yield a fat, little trout or two were barren, and I was hard put to it to get enough for our breakfasts. The thing was a mystery. I could not have caught them all. There were at least three miles of water that I fished, and the ten trout or so that I had taken daily surely could not have exhausted it. Thinking that they might have run upstream with the September rains, I decided to follow.

The lumber road followed the stream for perhaps two miles, crossing it again and again on rough log bridges. It came to an end in a big clearing where the tree tops were heaped in an impenetrable tangle. It was useless to try to walk across that clearing. I had to follow the brook bed. Here was wilderness indeed. The ground was thick with

The brook caught all the light of the sky. As the shadow came into it, I saw the outline of the proud head and branching horns.

pine needles, the air fragrant with their smell. There was a pleasant thrill to this exploration. Here was the home of the wildcat and the lynx, and once, in the soft earth by the stream side, I saw the footprint of a bear. I felt little chills as I thought that I might be watched by unfriendly eyes, but the slight uneasiness gave the final zest that my adventure needed.

Then, at last, I came to a sun-lit opening in the forest, a wild meadow thick with grass. There had been a beaver dam there, and, as the animals had departed or been trapped out, their dam had broken and left this meadow, rich with silt, as their monument. The brook here flowed silently over a bed of sand and gravel, the water perhaps six inches deep. I saw what appeared to be many sticks on the stream bed, but all were lying in the same direction facing up stream. Curious, I lay flat on my stomach in the lush grass and peered into the water. There were my missing trout! The water swarmed with little chaps of five or six inches, up to one or two lunkers over a foot long. They were spawning, and, in that clear water, the whole mystery of their reproduction was disclosed. With their fins and noses, they made little hollows in the gravel. The females took their positions over these hollows, the males swimming around them excitedly. The eggs were deposited, fertilized by the males, and the gravel fanned over them. I forgot fishing.

The long grass quite concealed me and, to avoid disturbing the trout, I was motionless. From across the brook came stealthy sounds. I raised my eyes. Not more than fifty feet away, a young buck was feeding at the edge of the woods. He would take a mouthful of grass, flip his white tail, raise his head, look around. Nose, ears, and eyes all were alert to warn him of danger. Never had I seen a wild deer so close. I trembled with excitement as I watched him. I was down wind from him, and he was unsuspecting. Then he threw his head into the air, ears and nose twitching, and faded into the forest. From that moment, I had an ambition, an object in life. As a successful hunter of big game, I felt I might attain the status of a school celebrity.

Downstream the meadow ended where the hills and the forest on both sides came almost together. The brook poured through this narrow defile, and became a wild, foaming torrent. Across this bottle neck lay the peeled trunk of a big tree, which had collected a mass of driftwood. Here was a perfect blind. Hidden behind it, I could command that meadow, and, given the chance, I felt that the little buck would be mine. From that day on I haunted the spot. Fishing forgot, I would take the rifle with me, steal up to the shelter of the fallen tree, peer eagerly through the tangle of driftwood, and settle down to wait for the buck. Day after day I lay in wait but, though each morning the meadow showed fresh tracks, I did not see their maker.

Then I concluded that he was feeding either early in the morning or in the evening. I tried getting there before sunrise, but was always too late. I waited until sundown, but had to leave too early, for I had no desire to come down that brook through the forest after dark.

Could any buck possibly be worth the terrors of a night alone in the woods? Riley refused to have any part of it. "What? Leave a bed so warm to shiver so foolishly in the wet woods? *Mais non, non!*" Riley snapped his fingers with a "Pouf!" I mentally did the same thing. Would I do it *alone? Mais non!*

The red and yellow leaves that had painted the maples were gone. Each night there was frost. Each morning we had to break the ice in the water pail. My vacation would soon be ended. In four more days I must say good-by to the amiable Riley and our snug log cabin. Let the little buck add more points to his horns. Perhaps he would still be there if I came up again. To show what I could do to him, I took the rifle, stuck a small envelope to the maple tree, and proceeded to

After a night of thrills Riley carried the little buck back to the cabin upon his shoulders, while I led with a lantern.

puncture it with five successive shots. Never had I shot so well. If I could shoot like that, was not the buck as good as mine? Why wait till next year?

Eagerness to become a big game hunter now outweighed my fears of the wilderness in the dark. I oiled my rifle, dressed in my warmest clothing, told Riley not to expect me until some time after dark, took my little flash light and a blanket, and set off upstream. In my pocket were two sandwiches and a bar of chocolate. I trembled with nervous excitement. I was embarking upon the first big adventure of my life.

Arriving at the fallen tree I found a rest for the rifle among the stubs of the branches, and left it there so that there would be less motion to alarm the deer when it should come time to aim. Then I seated myself upon the blanket to wait the coming of the deer.

The afternoon ended with a wintry sunset, and, in spite my two heavy sweaters, I shivered. The meadow darkened. All that I could see was the steely reflection of the sky in the brook. From the hill-side, a great horned owl hooted dismally, and my teeth began involuntarily to chatter. Far up the stream, from the blackness, came a long, savage, wavering cry. What it was I knew not, but I feared it was the howl of a wolf.

It was now between dusk and darkness. I heard new noises in the little meadow, such as a sheep makes when grazing. I strained my eyes to see. Surely there was a blacker shadow in the grass. Was it my imagination, or was there life in that shadow? I dared not fire at an uncertainty. I did not wish to experiment upon a bear for my first big game shooting. Was my long, cold, and fearsome wait to end fruitlessly because it was too dark to see my mark? I sat frozen, not daring to move, except to clutch my rifle, finger on trigger, in the hope it would be my buck. The shadow moved toward the brook and seemed to flow into it. What fortune! The brook caught all the little light of the sky, and, as the shadow entered it, I saw its outline clearly. There was a head held high, and on the head were horns!

I do not remember sighting the rifle. The moment of pulling the trigger was lost in the shock of the rifle's awful sound in the silence of the woods. The shadow disappeared even as I looked at it. With my youthful nerves shocked into a state of collapse, I sat behind the windfall, and trembled. I tried to summon courage to go with my flash light and see what had happened, but I could not.

Probably it was but a few moments later when I finally arose, though it seemed that the night must be far gone. I turned on my little flash light, and waded upstream to where the deer had been. There he was, motionless, hind legs in the water, body on the bank. My bullet had entered his left shoulder, and by the most fortunate chance had hit the heart. I had been told that it was necessary to bleed a deer after shooting, and I shuddered at what I must do. I pulled out Riley's long carving knife, which I had thought to bring, stuck it in where neck and chest joined, turned away my eyes and gagged. I wouldn't be fifteen until sunrise.

In my nervousness, I dropped the little flash light. I pawed around desperately in the grass and water trying to find it, but it had disappeared. I must go back to the camp through the darkness. I never can forget my frenzied dash downstream. It was a dash, too. I was frightened, and eager to get back to where there was light and human companionship. I took to the brook as offering the only certain road, and ran. I slammed into boulders, bounced from trees, went head-on into the log bridges, and fell on my face in the pools. My only comfort was that the noise I made would doubtless warn every bear and wildcat to get away.

Eventually, I panted into the lumber-camp clearing, and my heart bounded to see the windows aglow with light. I threw open the door. What my appearance was like I can guess, for Riley's eyes fairly popped from his head. "Come!" I gasped. "I've got him! Get the lantern, quick!"

Blessings upon that squat little Frenchman. He would have had reason to say, "Tomorrow is yet another day. We shall await it!" But, with rare understanding and sympathy, he lighted the lantern, put on his coat, and started back with me.

He carried that little buck back to the cabin upon his shoulders, I going ahead with the lantern. When he had dumped his load upon the floor of the cook house, we stood side by side and gazed long and silently at my trophy. When Riley spoke it was with proper respect and awe.

"Monsieur"—never before had I been *"monsieur"* to Riley— "is a shooter the most skilled. *Quelle bête!* What antlers. Here is a *trophée* the most *magnifique!"*

"How much will he weigh, Riley?" I asked, expanding my narrow chest. Riley looked judicial. He hefted the buck, just as though he had not already packed him over three miles. He did not rush into a conclusion so momentous.

"Tree ondred pound!" declared Riley.

Outdoor Life, April 1936

Wolf Dog

BY CHARLES ELLIOTT

L obo turned his black nose to the wind and loped into the twilight of the forest.

The air currents, woven together by threads of scent and sound, brought to his primitive senses a picture of the mountain woods ahead.

It set the scalp between his pointed ears to tingling. Here the world was new and strange.

John caught the puppy by the scruff of its neck and lifted it bodily.

He tasted the wind with a fierce exhilaration born of freedom and adventure.

Then suddenly the woods, which had been so fresh and clean, were filled with the reek of man. Lobo spun from his swinging lope and froze into a furry statue beside the trail. He stood through a moment of indecision, then turned and drifted like a dark shadow away from the path. He crouched where an ancient, mossback log pressed against the earth.

The human scent grew stronger. Out of the purple gloom that deepened where the trees were thick, the man appeared. His long stride brought him directly toward the log where the big wolf dog lay as taut as the string of a drawn bow.

A murderous growl died in Lobo's throat. His bleak straw-colored eyes clung to the booted human. The stick in John Livingston's hand was a symbol of authority and supremacy. But Lobo was ready. If the man paused suddenly and raised that stick to strike at him, he'd tear a human throat out with his steel-trap jaws.

John Livingston, however, did not pause or turn his head. He wondered vaguely why the hackles on his neck should tingle unpleasantly, but he strode on and faded into the dusk. The sound of his boots on the rocky trail grew faint. Once more the air was clean of human stench.

Minutes after the man had gone, Lobo rose warily. He did not take the trail again, but turned into the mountain woods which sloped sharply up to Balsam Ridge. A game trail climbed the crest of the ridge to Eagle Point. He padded across the rocky pinnacle and stood on its barren tip. The wind blew full and hard against him. Beyond the point the earth fell into opaque darkness. The broad, deep valley at his feet glinted with spots of silver where Eagle River sliced through the hills. An amber globe of moon hung on the violet rim beyond the valley.

The blood raced wild through Lobo's body. Man had tamed his eager muscles and forced knowledge into his stubborn brain, but had not been able to conquer his spirit. From this night on, no man would ever be his master.

This exciting new life sprang from a dramatic clash between the wolf dog and his master. Behind him were centuries upon centuries of wildness and fierceness which transformed him into a raging killer. Through generations of carefully bred and highly trained champions, the brutal wolf strain had lain dormant, waiting for such a dog as Lobo.

He had been the largest in a litter of six Alsatians. He was whelped in the purple, a line-bred descendant of Hamilton Anne Von Kruger, the finest strain of German shepherd dogs in the world. But Lobo was not a dog. He was a wolf. He was a product of that phenomenon by which shepherd dogs occasionally bring forth a true wolf from which their breed originated.

John Livingston knew he had a wolf cub in the litter. He watched the young puppy stand on legs so wobbly that they would scarcely support his weight and hoist his tiny black muzzle into the wind, while the other puppies lay curled up, asleep. The wolf dog puppy strutted across the kennel yard and stuck his long mouth into the water pan. Instead of lapping like a dog, he sucked up the water just as any member of a wild pack would have done.

John pushed open the gate and stepped into the pen. Lobo backed into a corner, a ball of fur on buckling legs, and growled. The breeder laughed. He caught the puppy by the scruff of its neck and lifted it into his arms. He stroked the silky hair between the tiny ears.

"I have a weakness for outlaws," he said, "or you'd get the guillotine."

John Livingston's eyes glowed at his discovery. He'd known men who had found wolf cubs in a litter. He had never believed they could be trained. George Cuvier once wrote how a wolf raised in the Jardin des Plantes in Paris had become fanatically devoted to its master. John scoffed at that, too, but the experiment was worth a trial. If he could harness all the vibrant fire and courage in such an animal, he'd have the champion dog of the world.

From the moment his eyes opened on his thirteenth day, Lobo was a malicious little brute with an ugly temper. Before he could stand on his stubby legs, he tried to chew the foot off a sister puppy. His mother cuffed him into a corner of the pen. He did not cry or whine. Instead, he growled defiance.

Lobo was weaned two weeks before his litter mates quit suckling. John brought a piece of red meat into the kennel and held it down before the pups. Only Lobo scented it. He rushed forward, tore the meat from his master's hand, and dragged it to a corner of the pen where he crouched and ripped the steak apart with gusty greed.

Several months after he was born, Lobo almost lost his head. It was not exactly his own fault, but it helped contribute to his general delinquency.

John's five-year-old daughter, Mary, had been told never to enter the pen of the Alsatians, and that order from her father, of course, made the kennel the most intriguing spot in the yard. When no one was looking, she worked at the heavy hasp which held the gate shut while the dogs watched her in indolent curiosity.

One day she gave the hasp an extra twist and the gate came open in her hand. Half fearfully, Mary stepped inside. Janie, Lobo's huge, dark mother, rose slowly to her feet, stretched, and sniffed at the little girl. Then she went back to her straw bed in the corner.

For the first time Lobo could not restrain the wild freedom in his heart. He gave voice and his running cry swelled upward through the night.

The puppies surged toward her, tumbling around her feet; all except Lobo, who lay by the fence and never took his eyes away from the girl. Being a female, and human, the little girl waded through the furry shepherd pups to Lobo, the one who showed no sign of affection for her. She stooped to stroke the wolf dog's silky hair, and he snapped at her hand, his needle teeth scratching her chubby fingers.

Mary stumbled backward in surprise and lost her balance. She fell sprawling on the ground and instantly Lobo was upon her, growling and biting at her ankles. The other puppies, sensing some kind of a new game, tumbled over her and one of them pushed Lobo away. Janie, who had watched John Livingston roll her progeny around affectionately, looked on with sleepy eyes.

The little girl, badly frightened, managed to scramble to her feet and run to the gate. She did not try to put the hasp back in place. John Livingston found her half hidden under the rose bush at the front steps, her face wet with tears. He picked her up in his arms.

"What's the matter, honey?" he asked.

She told him in broken sentences, pointing out Lobo and the half-closed gate. For a long minute the man studied Lobo with thoughtful eyes.

"When you bother the dogs," he said quietly to his daughter, "they might hurt you. I'd punish Lobo if he had tried to bite you without teasing, but it was your fault and not his."

"I hate him," said the little girl.

Lobo, sensing the spirit behind her words, growled softly. Some day he would find Mary alone. His yellow eyes grew red around the rims.

John Livingston spent hours with Lobo each day. He was so fascinated by the wolf dog that he neglected the other puppies. Against the wishes of the young savage, he taught him to heel and charge and fetch a thrown ball.

Lobo found one bright spot in his training. He looked forward to those times when his master carried him into the woods with their deep glades and sun-splotched forest floors. Once John lost him for an hour and found him stalking a big cottontail, almost as large as the pup. The rabbit bounced away when John appeared and picked Lobo up in his arms.

"You little pagan," he said. "If that had been a coon or an otter, I probably would have found you without a scalp."

They ranged together frequently in Cooper's Cove. This primitive upland forest lay in the big bend of Eagle River. There the oaks and hickories were huge and formed a canopy so thick that no sunlight ever touched the ground. The cove was a favorite haunt of the Russian wild boars, recently introduced into the Southern mountains. The extensive woods, carpeted with leaves and decaying vegetation, were similar to their home in the Old World and provided delicate tidbits of acorns and mushrooms and tender shoots.

John and the puppy stumbled upon the herd one day. Lobo hurtled down the slope and charged a huge black boar that stood almost three feet at the shoulder and weighed more than an eighth of a ton. The boar, more in amazement than antagonism, swung to face the gangling puppy. His head went down and before Lobo could sidestep he caught the dog a glancing blow that bowled him ten feet into the leaves.

Ignoring the danger to himself, Livingston raced downhill and scooped the puppy up into his arms. While the boar hesitated, rumbling in its throat, the man clawed his way to safety in the granite cliffs with Lobo twisting in his arms to free himself and make another attack.

John Livingston sewed up the cut in the puppy's shoulder. Two inches either way and the stiletto tusk would have cut off the young life almost before it had begun. But the experience only served to instill in Lobo a hatred for any creature that smelled like a hog. He was certain that without his master's interference he could have put the clumsy boar back on its haunches. Out of his confidence grew a challenge to the whole pig tribe. His hackles rose like brown wires when he found a split track in the earth and the bitter smell of swine blew to his nose.

When he was locked in his pen, Lobo paced the sides like a caged wild beast, searching for some means of escape. His litter mates were content to lie in the sun. He tested the fence with his teeth, or tried to dig away the concrete floor. He worked periodically at a loose board under the gate. One day when he pushed at the plank trying to get his nose out, it came loose at one end. Lobo did not hesitate. Sensing freedom, he pushed through, leaving a tuft of hair on the sharp nail.

He half circled the pen, thinking of the mountain woods which lay across the meadow. Then he saw Mary, playing at her favorite spot under the rosebush. She was upwind and her smell brought back the memory of that day in the pen. He crouched on his belly, watching her. He slunk within a dozen yards of the girl, his yellow eyes gleaming. Then he lay motionless. It wasn't knowledge or experience that kept him from hurting the little girl. It was instinct, a thousand generations old, that told him death would be his penalty for an attack on this man child.

So taut were his muscles, so intent his concentration, that he did not hear John Livingston walk into the yard. He came alive when the heavy step was over him. He sprang forward, too late. The man's iron fist was in the scruff of his neck. He snarled and fought when John lifted him bodily off the ground and broke a switch from the apple tree in the yard. The lashes stung his sides and legs and back, but Lobo did not whine or cry out. He fought silently to free himself, but the man was too strong.

Beads of sweat stood on John's forehead when he opened the gate and dropped Lobo back into the pen. "If I could read your mind," he said, grimly, "I'd probably kill you. But, by gad, I'll break you if it makes an old man of me."

Lobo did not realize that those incidents had become a part of him. He did not know it months later when he lay flattened on the kennel floor. But the first taste of the autumn wind was like sweet perfume to his nose, and every nerve and muscle was a-tingle when John Livingston opened the gate to put on his training collar.

Lobo suddenly changed from an apparently sleeping dog to a flash of gray. He was gone before the man could slam the gate again. The dog whistle shrilled. Lobo knew it was a command for him to return, and he stopped to look back, ears pointed the sky. Training was strong, but not so strong as his instinct for freedom. He swept over the brow of the low hill that bordered the Livingston fields and headed at a dead run up the river trail. Later he left the trail and cut across the pastured acres of Jeremiah Duke who owned the farm across the creek.

This morning Lobo was only in a playful mood. He intended to make a short circle of a few miles and return to the pen where his master would be waiting. During the months of kindness and patience he had almost forgotten the whipping he received for stalking little Mary in the front yard. He learned fast and John always rewarded him with a piece of meat when he was obedient. So he turned back toward the house.

He was running fast when he crossed the corner of the Duke pasture and his sensitive nostrils swelled with the hated smell of swine. He wheeled and cut back through a clump of trees, following that scent.

He was in the middle of the pigs almost before he saw them. The thicket exploded and bawling shoats took off toward all points of the pasture. In sheer exuberance, Lobo leaped after one of the terrified animals, slashing at its hamstrings, much as a member of a wild pack would have done. The pig went down, bellowing in mortal terror. Lobo lunged for its throat. His teeth cut the bellow to a gasp and hot blood splashed into his eyes.

He ran to earth and killed another shoat before he heard the pound of running feet and saw Jeremiah Duke angling across the field. The big dog swung and sprinted for the protection of the trees. The roar behind him kicked up gravel that stung through his heavy coat.

Lobo gained the shelter of the woods before the farmer shot again. His native intelligence told him that he was in danger and the only protection he knew was in the Livingston kennel yard. He fled across the slopes and crept through the gate his master had left open.

Duke was with John Livingston when they found him there, crouched in a corner, his eyes blazing. The farmer's face was red. John Livingston's white knuckles were tight around a stick. He dragged Lobo out by the nape of the neck and rubbed hog hair against his nose. Then he struck the wolf dog with his stick. He

Two men dressed in green forest-ranger uniforms stopped a few feet from Lobo. The wolf dog lay on his belly and waited, seemingly friendly and whining gently, but with every muscle like a steel spring.

rubbed the hated smell in the dog's nostrils a second time and belted him in the loins.

"I hate to do this, old man," he said, "but you've got to learn sometime."

The wolf dog lunged and twisted with all the power of his young shoulders to tear out of his master's hand, but the grip in those fingers was too firm.

John raised his stick a third time, but a vicious jerk of the young demon threw the man off balance and he went down, losing his hold. Lobo did not hesitate. He plunged at his sprawling master's throat. But Duke was quicker than the dog. He swung his broad boot. It caught Lobo full in the face and knocked him against the kennel fence. The wolf dog leaped again. John Livingston, staggering to his feet, struck with the stick. Lobo met it in his lunge and went down with the breath knocked out of his body. John jumped forward to catch the dog again, but Lobo bolted past him through the gate. He ran with long, low strides toward the big woods that climbed the slope beyond the river.

"He's a killer," Jeremiah Duke said, his big hand propped against the kennel fence.

John Livingston did not reply. In all his years as a trainer, he had never seen such spirit in a dog. He had almost met sudden death under Lobo's teeth, and he should have been glad to have the young devil out of his kennel. But somehow, deep inside, he felt a curious loss, for he knew that Lobo would never come home again.

Now the moon was swinging clear into the blackened sky and stars were popping out in the dome that arched over Windy Mountain. Lobo picked his way down the rocky slope and struck the forest trail that led into the laurel canyons where he and his master had often ranged together. There was no regret and no fear in his heart.

Halfway across the slope he nosed through a thicket and jumped a rabbit. The cottontail tumbled down the mountain like a leaping rubber ball. Lobo could have caught it in two easy bounds, but instead he loped along at an easy gait, following the hot scent that spread along the sweet bosom of the earth. Life was full and overflowing, and for the first time Lobo could not restrain the wild freedom in his heart. He gave voice and his running cry swelled upward through the night.

Far down in the valley, John Livingston stood up with half an arm-load of firewood. He had heard wolves in the arctic wastes and knew the hunting cry of the pack. In that faint, trailing sound he could sense the spirit Lobo felt, a spirit not to be denied by chains and wire and leather collar bands. The wolf dog had gone back to the wilderness which was his own, but in which he was now an evil influence. He must be hunted down and killed.

Mid-fall had spread its myriad colors in the Southern mountains. Lobo was fully grown. He stood more than two feet high at the shoulders and weighed almost as much as a man. The puppy black had disappeared from his body. His nose sat like a lump of wet coal at the end of his light-gray muzzle. His belly fur was creamy white. His back was dusky brown that blended on his flanks to gray and copper.

He had the lean and narrow muzzle of a true wolf. It swelled into a broad forehead and powerful jaws. His oblique eyes had lightened to the straw color of dead winter grass.

Lobo's home was a rocky cave under the summit of Windy Mountain. Below his den the ridges and coves spread out like a wrinkled relief map. This vast, wild upland, cradled in the heart of the southern Appalachians, was the finest game country in the region. Deer, bears, and smaller game were abundant. In its heart, Uncle Sam's foresters and game men had created a 50,000-acre game refuge. They had established a control program for foxes and wildcats and set up plans to maintain nature's balance of all the forest creatures. The appearance of Lobo was a menace to their plans.

Each day the big wolf dog dozed on the granite stoop at the entrance to his den. At night, from dusk until dawn flamed in the sky, he ranged the forest for sport and food. Sometimes he hunted in late afternoon when the wind was cold and his muscles were restless and tired.

Lobo's greatest sport was with the bears. These big black animals had grown more plentiful in the protected refuge, year by year. His first encounter with one of them came early one morning as he loafed back from a hunt along the river. He was loping along a game trail that led under a precipice when he came face to face with the bear. It reared up and put its nose to the wind. It was the largest animal Lobo had ever met in the woods. Caution, not fear, rumbled softly in the wolf dog's chest. His full scent reached the bruin's nose, and the creature wheeled and fled back up the trail. Lobo smashed after it, giving excited tongue. He remained a safe distance behind because those hairy paws were huge and had the power of dealing sudden destruction.

They ran only a short distance and the bear treed in an oak with limbs close to the ground. Lobo sat at the foot of the tree and looked up curiously. He could not understand why so huge a creature was a coward. The bear, with one leg over a large branch, cocked its head and watched the wolf dog in a comical manner.

After an hour of circling the tree and barking spasmodically, Lobo grew tired of the sport and trotted on up the trail to his den. But from that moment on, he never failed to chase any of the bruins he met in the woods.

Of all the creatures in the mountain forest, Lobo despised only the boars. The spoor of pigs deep in the coves raised his hunting hackles and bared his rapier teeth.

One day at dusk he padded along a mountain trail that led him into Cooper Cove beyond where Eagle River thundered down its gorge. His nose discovered pig scent in the air. The herd was stomping along the forest floor, snuffling in the leaves for acorns and sweet roots.

The wolf circled a laurel clump and crouched there until they fed almost beneath him on the cove floor. One enormous bound carried him into the herd, snapping, snarling, roaring in his throat. The sows and shoats scampered to safety up the cove, and Lobo found himself surrounded by three of the ugliest pigs he had ever seen. They had little black eyes as wicked as his own and bright ivory tusks that curled up out of lower jaws. They had no idea of running away from a fight.

Lobo's eyes caught the flash of yellow light that came from the back door of the house. The farmer stood there, peering out into the moonlight.

One of the wild hogs lowered his head and charged. Lobo twisted away and doubled back, catching the pig behind its ear, clamping down with jaws that brought a squall of pain. A sharp stab in the flank made him snap his head around. He set his teeth and ripped off an ear.

The other boars were at his rear, cutting his flanks to ribbons with dagger tusks. Lobo leapt away and fled up the mountain. It was not bravery or cowardice. The odds against him were too great. Some day he'd meet one of those big hogs alone, and then his debt would be paid in full.

He loped on up the cove. The sun had gone. The trees blazed iridescent in the twilight and the forest aisles were thick with falling autumn leaves. The thunder of Balsam Falls grew loud, then dim again against his ears. He came into the upper cove, a silent cathedral of pillared oaks and poplars.

Deer scent sweetened the air. Lobo slunk to his belly. Two does with half-grown fawns nosed along the game trail of the cove. He stalked them, silent as a shadow of the stars, upwind so they could not scent him. He sprang before the deer were aware of death. He dragged down a fawn. The other animals in the little herd bounced away on startled slender legs.

Lobo feasted well. He preferred the heart and lungs and liver to the hot rump steaks. Dawn found him curled in a hollow tree, high on the ridge. There he languished through the day. When night came his nerves and muscles lost their listlessness. He circled the ridge and traveled back to the cove. He planned to make a second meal from the carcass of the deer, but as he approached the kill, his eager nose was stuffy with the bitter scent of humans.

Lobo stopped full in his stride. He circled warily, distrustful of all man-made smells. He found a spot where the leaves had been disturbed and then rearranged. Out of curiosity he pawed gently at the leaves with his big foot. The ground gleamed bright under the leaf layer. He stuck out his forepaw timidly to touch the silvery object, and it suddenly leaped at him, snapping tight shut on the end of his paw.

Lobo tumbled backward, but too late. He bit at the trap, but the bright steel was more savage than his own jaws. It cut his lips and teeth. He lunged again, twisting, turning, jerking, trying to tear his paw away, but the steel only snagged more viciously into his flesh.

Blood trickled down where he cut his jaws. The leaves and black earth were mutilated where he had braced himself and pulled until he howled from sheer anguish. Then suddenly the big dog lay down beside the trap and let his cunning take over the madness which flashed warning signals in his brain.

John Livingston would finally come for him. John had punished him before and the heavy stick against his hide would never be as terrible as trying to tear his foot away, as useless as wasting his strength on a lifeless and inexorable antagonist.

For the remainder of the night Lobo lay with his head on his free paw, fighting back the impulse to struggle against that gray steel which held him helpless. His blood ran sluggish and his woolly coat quivered from the cold. His foot, which had been hot with pain, grew numb with a slow dull throb. He moved it and the agony came again, so he lay still against the cold earth and waited. The first lesson of the wild is patience, and he was to learn it well.

Twilight passed, dawn came, and the stars in the sky winked out one by one. The dead leaves around him stirred in the morning wind that rose with the sun. The sunlight was yellow and cold and made faint shadows against the earth. Then his quick ears caught the pad of human feet on the mountain.

Lobo beat back an impulse to spring to his feet and tear out of the trap. His first instinct was the instinct of life, and he had not lived by strength alone. The human steps came closer, but he did not recognize the gangling stride of John Livingston. There were two men instead of one. He lay on his belly and waited, seemingly at ease, but every muscle was like a coiled steel spring.

The two men stopped a few feet from him. They were dressed in green and wore wide-brimmed hats. Their eyes were staring in amazement.

"Why," one said, "it's just a big police dog."

"It may be that wolf," the other replied skeptically. "Better kill him."

Some strength greater than his mad impulses made Lobo whine gently in his throat.

"It's nothing but a dog, Joe," the first ranger stated again.

He leaned his rifle against a tree and stood over Lobo. The wolf dog was breathing fast now, but somehow he knew that his very life depended on not tearing off the hand that stroked the fur between his ears, much as John Livingston had done.

Joe knelt beside his fellow ranger and together the two men pried apart the jaws of the trap. The pain was sharp once more when Joe lifted out the mangled paw and Lobo's whine was genuine. The ranger pulled the trap away and bent over to pick the dog up in his arms, but Lobo was not there. One moment he was a pitiable creature, the next a flash of fur threading the forest aisles. He was gone before the startled ranger could jump for his gun.

Joe took off his hat and rubbed his forehead. "Don't ever tell the chief about this," he said. "We'd be sunk."

Lobo made his tortuous way through the forest and climbed the ridge to his den. There he lay in the sunshine and brooded with his eyes watching the ridges and a pair of hawks that circled beyond the cliffs above their aerie.

In the days that followed, Lobo's foot healed slowly. The trap had left a permanent scar in the big foot, but he soon lost his limp and was running with his old stamina through the forest. His hatred for mankind was bitter, and he avoided all taint of human smells. He found fresh sheep liver laid carelessly in the woods and walked around it, even though he had not made his kill. Sometimes he almost walked into a trap in the trail, or where a set of three or four traps had been made. The sign left by man when setting the steel snares were as plain as the sunrise in the east.

One day he found such a string of traps set in front of his den. He never returned to the den. His instinct for survival told him that the men had found his home. He moved to another rocky crevice in the high cliffs above Cooper Cove.

The wolf dog killed when he wanted food and occasionally for the sport of killing. He became the terror of all the mountain forest. When his hunting bark rang down the coves, the forest creatures shuddered in their beds and den trees. He never went hungry. The woods were full of deer and rabbits and mice, and sometimes he treed a raccoon or an opossum for sport, much as a trained hunting dog would have done.

Spring came to the mountains and to the ridges that climbed up from the valleys. The buds of maple trees swelled and burst in fiery red. The poplars by the streams were amber green, and new leaves on the oak trees looked like squirrel ears. The warm winds and rains painted the forest with a bright new emerald, and hordes of flitting birds filled the woods with color and song.

Lobo stood at the door of his rocky den, his feet braced against the stone step that bulwarked the empty space beyond. A ravenous desire, not born of appetite or hatred, burned in his deep chest. It puzzled him, annoyed him, gleamed in his amber eyes. Somewhere from far beyond the ridges, as straight and true as a swallow to its cliff nest, the call had come to him. It was mating time.

Before the sun went down, Lobo left the cove and traveled the ridge trail to the high knob above Eagle River. The sky grew black, and yellow lights appeared like pinpoints in the valley. The call was there, where she was waiting, somewhere in the bottom lands beyond the river.

He ran swiftly down the ridge to Eagle River. The water was fast and cold, but he scarcely felt the chill on his trembling hide. He was following a hunger not born of empty vitals. It led him to Jeremiah Duke's house beside the tumbling creek.

A yellow light burned in the window of the house and Lobo circled cautiously. The call was in a shed that sloped off from the big barn 100 feet beyond the kitchen steps. The wolf dog crept up on his belly and stuck his muzzle into one of the cracks that ran the length of the shed wall. The crack was wide enough for vision. Locked inside was a beautiful collie, the loveliest creature he had ever seen. She stepped timidly forward and touched his black nose with hers.

Lobo explored the three sides of the shed, examining the walls minutely. He dug into the hard earth, but the floor was concrete on stone foundation. The collie whined softly, eagerly, setting his blood on a wild sweep through his body. He found a shaky board and thrust the upper part of his jaw into the crack. He set his teeth and threw his raw-boned weight against the plank. The shed was old and the piece of timber tore away, snapping like a pistol.

In a savage shower of splinters the hole grew larger. The collie, her nose almost touching him, was crying now in her fervor and impatience. Lobo worked feverishly, tearing out mouthfuls of the hard wood, wrecking the shed in his throes of anticipation and desire.

Suddenly his eyes caught the flash of yellow light that flooded from the back door of the house. The farmer stood, looking out into the moonlight.

"Hand me my gun quick, Sarah," he said. "There's something trying to git in the shed. It's as big as that wolf dog."

He ran into the yard and Lobo whirled. With lust burning in his throat he half faced the man. But the fear of humans had become a deeply rooted part of him. He spun and took off through the yard. He leaped to clear the high fence that marked the garden.

The roar of the farmer's gun blasted in his ears and his shoulder was almost torn out of the socket. The bullet knocked him completely over in the air and threw him on his back beyond the garden fence. He rolled to his feet as the gun roared again. The lead ball pelted dirt into his face.

Lobo fled remarkably fast with one leg dangling uselessly. He raged inside. He stifled a mad desire to circle back and attack the farmer from behind. But he was powerless against guns and clubs and his desire for survival was the most impelling sense of all.

His leg pounded in agony. This injury obliterated the whippings and the steel trap. He stopped and licked at the dripping blood. The bullet had torn through flesh and ligaments, and when he threw his weight against the foot his eyes went black with pain. He circled the river trail and climbed the long ridge to the head of Cooper Cove. There he lay down and soothed the torn muscles with his tongue.

Jeremiah Duke stood in the Livingston back yard, his gun still under his arm.

"I busted that wolf hard when he went over my back fence," he said. "I found blood where he hit the ground. He can't travel very fast or very far."

"Then it's killing time for that son of a dog," John Livingston said. His words were hard and crisp, but the farmer thought he could detect a note of resignation in his neighbor's voice.

"You finish your supper," Livingston said, "and I'll go after Buck Simpson's hounds in the truck. If Lobo's bad wounded, we won't have trouble finding him or running him to earth on the mountain."

An hour later Lobo heard dogs bellowing far below in the fields. They found his blood on the forest leaves and announced their find in a ringing chorus. They trailed up the slope and Lobo pushed himself erect on his three sound feet. The pain in his leg spread through his other muscles and left them tight.

Normally Lobo would have fled, giving the hounds the race of their lives before he left them far behind on a lost trail. But he was grim and wounded tonight. He limped painfully 200 yards along the ridge crest, then doubled back, crouched beside a granite boulder, and waited.

The dogs came on, singing their melodious song of the trail. They struck his fresh scent and leapt ahead with frenzied tongues. They approached the wolf dog's ambush by the cliff. Lobo struck hard and fast. His useless leg was more than compensated by savage anger. He swept out of the shadows, into the pack, snarling and slashing. The first hound died with a bellow still in its throat. A second Walker swung to face him. The wolf dog cut it to a mangled heap before the look of surprise went off its face.

The big, flop-eared dogs were not fighters. The remaining dog leaped away and then came back, yelling at the top of its voice, telling the humans down the ridge that it had treed. Lobo jumped at the dog but it sprang out of range. It turned and bayed again.

The sound of running human feet beat through the woods. Lobo turned to sprint away and the hound swept after him with triumphant tones. But the wolf dog did not run. He snapped around and seized the hound at the base of its throat. He swung his head just once and the dog rolled over, quivering in the agony of a violent death.

Lobo climbed the jumbled heap of rocks. He crouched on top of the cliff with his face toward the area he had left. He was safe here. Human eyes could not see him in the dark. Human noses could not follow his trail.

The light from the lantern in Jeremiah Duke's hand glinted on the bodies of the dead hounds. His gnarled hand tightened slowly around the gun.

"Gad!" said John Livingston softly, "what a brute."

He unsnapped the bloody collars from the dogs, and the men stalked back down the trail, the shadows of their legs like monstrous spiders against the earth.

When they had gone beyond the range of his ears, Lobo arose and limped a weary mile up the mountain, where he crawled into a laurel thicket and sank down on a mattress of drifted leaves. There he lay for the remainder of the night and throughout the next day, alternately sleeping and licking the bullet wound in his shoulder.

The afternoon was waning fast when Lobo crawled out of the laurel thicket and stood erect. He could not put his foot down without pain stabbing through his muscles and nerves into his very brain. His eyes were bloodshot and the broad muscles ached across his chest. He had no desire to hunt, but his insides were complaining loudly at the lack of food.

He nosed along a thicket and jumped a rabbit at the forks of the Eagle trail. He sprang, but with the injured foreleg, landed at an awkward angle and missed. He threw out his game foot to catch his weight. When it touched the ground, an explosion of pain burned through his body. The leg buckled under him and he rolled over into the leaves.

All the wolf dog's ill temper flared into flame. He was diabolic. He raged down the forest trail into Cooper Cove, traveling fast on three legs, his eyes bloodshot and mad with the terrible punishment of his wound. The cold river was somewhere below him. He would find the icy water and submerge himself in it to drive out the fevered torment.

Suddenly he stumbled in his stride. His nostrils were full of human scent and the scent of a bear, all mixed up in one foul odor. The flat crack of a gun and a muffled human yell filled the forest. Lobo stood suddenly on a low knoll that rose above the broad floor of the cove.

Before him John Livingston lay sprawled on the ground. It was the second time he had ever seen his old master down. His leg was twisted at an ugly angle, his gun half buried in the leaves where it had been knocked out of his hands. Standing almost over the man was a huge black bear, with blood flowing out of its side.

Lobo did not see the two cubs scrambling for safety up the broad beam of a white oak. He did not know that John had surprised the mother bear and startled her so that she charged instinctively to protect her cubs. He only saw man, his enemy, helpless on the ground. His feverish brain was beyond reason, with only the unquenchable desire to kill. He did not hesitate. He charged downhill as fast as his three good legs would keep him upright.

The bear heard his padded feet in the leaves and swung to face this new menace to her cubs. Lobo was suddenly conscious that she was not running away, as had the other bears he'd treed. The big, ungainly creature had the temerity to stand up to him.

Instinct and the knowledge of fight had been born in the wolf dog. Momentarily he forgot John Livingston. He held his ground until the bear had thundered down almost upon him, then hurtled aside. He snapped at the white patch on her throat and missed. She spun in her tracks and ripped Lobo with her long claws. The dog swerved, but his weak leg folded under him and he half fell. The bear ripped open a long gash in his hide and his ribs stood white and bare, then streaked with red.

The blow knocked Lobo around, his head close to the broad ham of his foe. He snapped his teeth shut on the black thigh where the hamstrings were, crushing through fur and flesh to the sinews. The bear squalled in pain.

Lobo's mighty jaws closed tighter until the broad haunch gave way. Then one of the bear's flailing paws sent him rolling. She whirled on her good legs to face the wolf dog.

Lobo saw John Livingston crawling toward the gun. He knew that he must finish this first battle quickly and reach the man before the gun was in his hands. He forgot everything but the certain knowledge that he was fighting for his life.

He lashed in savagely, thrusting his head right and left. With his injured leg he could not maneuver quickly, so he traded blow for blow, thrust for counterthrust. The bear was fighting a short, furious battle. Her own hindquarter was useless. The bullet wound in her side was gnawing at her life.

Lobo, himself, was bleeding to death. Salty blood was in his eyes and nose. Through the blur he saw that John Livingston was trying to point the gun, but the conflict raged too fast in its whirl of flying bodies.

With all his reserve power Lobo charged, and his grip of death closed on the bear's thick throat while Livingston struggled to aim his rifle.

"Fight her, Lobo!" He heard the words through dimming senses. "Fight her!"

Lobo could not run now. With all his reserve power he feinted twice and charged. His grip of death closed on the thick throat and blood spurted in his face. The bear shook with tremendous power, but Lobo held. She beat at him with ham-like paws, but his grip was the grip of death. The big black bear sank slowly down upon her belly.

The wolf dog freed his jaws from her throat and turned on unsteady legs to face the man. He could not see through the red mist that closed his eyes. His head was spinning but he lunged toward the human voice for his second kill. The man's voice was far away.

"Lobo! Lobo! Here, boy!"

He staggered forward to lash out with bloody jaws. He collapsed and his outstretched head, grinning in its malevolent purpose, fell into John Livingston's hands. The life went out of him. His great body shuddered convulsively and relaxed into oblivion.

Tears streamed down John Livingston's face. He laid the big head across his knee and stroked it gently with his finger tips. Words flooded out of his heart, but he could not speak. Lobo had come back to him, had given his own life for his master. There could be no greater test of a champion, no greater sacrifice for a friend.

Outdoor Life, October 1947

The Gift

BY VIN T. SPARANO

I wanted Matt to have a gift that would last as long as he lived.

I watched the whitetail cautiously cross the field in high grass. I didn't know if it was a buck or doe, but it was heading for the hedgerow where I had placed my son.

Did Matt see the deer? If it was a buck, was he ready to accept what he was about to do? Was age 15 too young to be on a deer stand alone?

I could not see Matt, but then I heard the shot and saw the four-pointer down in the clearing between the field and the hedgerow. When I reached my son, he was standing over his first buck.

I had taught Matt all I knew about deer hunting. I had explained the rut and showed him rubs and scrapes. I had told him about scents and tree stands. But I never really believed that I could prepare him for his first big-game hunt. Young Matt reacted as I had many many years earlier. At first, he was quiet. I knew every thought coursing through his mind. Words could never adequately describe the seriousness and sensitivity of what you have just done. Then comes the elation and the acceptance of your deer as a gift from whomever it is you choose to believe in . . .

This afternoon, 13 years and at least as many deer camps later, I was glassing for elk in a huge golden meadow in New Mexico. I watched Matt, now a man of 28, and Travis Benes, his guide, as they hunted the meadow ahead of me. Like the day of that first whitetail, long ago, this afternoon Matt was trying for his first elk.

I had hunted the same basin the night before with Dr. Dick Gooding, the New Mexico plastic surgeon who owns the ranch. We had stayed until dark, keeping a dozen cows in sight for at least two hours. Just as we were about to get up and leave, a bull bugled no more than 50 yards behind us in the heavy timber bordering the meadow.

With only about 10 minutes of shooting light left, I had no choice but to work toward the bull. When I got into the timber, however, I realized that I had miscalculated the remaining light. It was pitch-dark—and then the bull bugled again. He sounded as if he was right in front of me! I had no intention of confronting that bull in the dark and backed off.

Today, Matt and his guide were having the same kind of luck—except this time, they had an audience. I was sitting about 20 yards behind Matt and Travis. My old friend and *Outdoor Life* Hunting Editor Jim Zumbo was watching from a ridge behind me. Just as they had done the night before, the cows came off the ridge and fed slowly into the meadow. Once again, no bull followed.

As we waited there, silent in the fading light, every second of the hunt for Matt's first deer 13 long years ago came rushing back to me.

Like that first whitetail, this elk hunt, too, would be something very special—my wedding present to Matt. At this time in his life, he did not have the money for an elk hunt, although money wasn't the real reason we were here in New Mexico together. As I grow older, these hunting trips become more and more important to me. I will need these memories.

We were here for five October days, and George Taulman of United States Outfitters had promised us an outstanding hunt. He kept his word. We had collected two bulls in two days. I took mine on a misty morning as we tried to get close to a herd of cows. We had moved no more than 100 yards, when Zumbo spotted a bull watching us stalk his herd. It was a heavy bull with a 5x6 rack. Later, Jim also got an elk, a five-pointer.

But Matt still waited for his elk—my wedding present. At first, perhaps making a wedding present of an elk sounds a little strange, but not if it's intended as a memory that two men will carry for the rest of their lifetimes.

Of course, Matt and I already shared the memory of many unforgettable hunts and fishing trips together. Some of these memories were tough, some frightening and some just plain bad. There was the time our bush plane blew an oil seal, and we were forced down at an

The ranch where we stayed and hunted on Chromo Mountain, New Mexico, near the Colorado border.

abandoned weather station near some unused railroad tracks in the Canadian bush. I found a couple of rusty rail spikes and gave one to Matt as a reminder in years to come of the sometimes unforgiving reality of wilderness areas. He was only 12, and I wondered whether the uncertainties of these remote adventures were wise for someone with a long, healthy life ahead of him.

But I felt no guilt about keeping Matt out of school for that trip. We lived with our Ojibway guides for eight days, and Matt experienced a way of life that can not be comprehended from a distant classroom.

On that same Canadian trip, I took a fish hook out of Matt's finger, using the loop of line technique for the first time. An hour or so later, he landed a 23-pound pike that once hung on a wall in my home. It is now on a wall in his home.

There were other hunting and fishing trips that went sour. Matt came fishing with me in a tournament one day before he was of driving age, and my 24-foot boat broke down 20 miles off the coast of New Jersey. No other boats were in sight, and I called in a Mayday to the Coast Guard—no simple trick when we discovered that the fuse connector on my radio was broken. I had to squeeze the connector in one hand while radioing our distress signal. The Coast Guard found us just before dark, after we'd fired nearly a dozen aerial flares.

We have all heard that a man's entire life can race through his mind when he is experiencing something extremely intense or life threatening. This must be true, because as I sat now in the intense silence of this New Mexico twilight, with Matt up ahead, waiting for his first elk, vivid memories were flooding my mind. Like the time when one of our Ojibway guides was struck in the head with a loose ax head, and Matt and I had to bandage him with duct tape and our shirts to keep him from bleeding to death. The guide had no radio, so we put him in a boat with another guide for a nine-hour trip to a base camp. Matt and I stayed behind in a trapper's cabin to wait for our plane, which didn't show up for two days because of bad weather. We fished, drank water from the lake and at night listened to the baby-like cry of a Canada lynx behind our cabin. Deciding at last that we were no threat, the lynx came right out and stared at us.

As the years pass, unpredictable adventures like those have become more meaningful to me than all the trips that came off without a hitch. And all of them together, the good and the hard, are part of the heritage that produces a person like Matt—a person who can take

Matt Sparano (left) and Vin Sparano with Matt's big bull.

care of himself in the outdoors . . . and a person who understands and respects the priceless values that only hunting and fishing can teach.

Matt and Travis were having the same problem I'd had the night before. The twilight was getting dimmer by the minute, and all they had in view were cows.

The sun was a finger of light at the top of the ridge across the meadow, its last rays casting a golden hue across the meadow. The ridge gleamed with the colors of flame. I tried to capture it on film, but the sound of the shutter seemed out of place during these magic moments.

When I saw Travis get up, I assumed it was time to return to the ranch. I stood up and started to stretch . . . but Travis wasn't getting ready to leave. He was trying to get more light into his binoculars.

Something was happening in the meadow. I got down quickly and looked through my binoculars in the near-darkness.

The big bull had just cleared the timber and was moving into the meadow. With each step, his huge rack swung from side to side. I lowered the glasses to see if Matt had also seen the bull, but he was already in position. He had his .300 Winchester Magnum already propped on a forked shooting stick.

I put my binoculars back on the bull and begged for just a minute or two more of shooting light.

When the massive bull turned broadside, Matt fired. The elk didn't move. I fought back the urge to shout, "Shoot again!"

But Travis had already whispered to Matt that his shot was a good one. As I watched, the bull's legs buckled. He went down.

Before I could say anything, the stillness was again shattered. This time it was Zumbo, who had also watched from the ridge behind me and was shouting, "Nice bull! Great shot! Nice bull!"

Matt and Travis were halfway to the bull before I could get to my feet and grab my pack and rifle. When we reached the bull, a distance of about 275 yards or so, darkness had settled in so deeply that we needed flashlights to get a close look at the elk.

He was a big six-point bull with a perfectly symmetrical rack. After hunting whitetails for so many years, the size of a mature bull elk is literally breathtaking. I guessed the weight at about 800 pounds.

Then, just as had happened 13 years ago, there was a quiet moment. Matt held the ivory-tipped rack in his hands and looked at his bull. And just as I did on our first deer hunt, I gave Matt a big bear hug.

Travis took out his knife to field-dress the elk, but Matt stopped him. I knew why. It was Matt's elk. The field-dressing would be his. In the glow of flashlights, Matt dressed the huge bull as we all watched.

The time will come—all too soon—when Matt will be putting his son on a deer stand for the first time. And he will know, as I did, that he is giving my grandson something very special . . . in fact, a gift that is priceless.

Outdoor Life, October 1994

Cougar Nightmare

By E. Boyd Hilderbrand
as told to Ken Crandall

The four lions that found my camp gave me no choice; I had to hunt all of them.

Blazing eyes and bared fangs, the cat came like a shot, nearly combing my whiskers with a hooking swipe.

I don't know how many times the cougar squalled before I finally woke up, but my awakening was certainly hastened by the realization that the cat was practically in bed with me.

I sat up and stared vainly into the snow-filled ring of darkness surrounding my dying campfire. Somewhere, just outside that flitting

black wall, a big cougar was watching me at a distance measured in feet. As a professional bounty hunter with nearly 40 cougar hides stretched out in the past few years, I felt no great fear. My only emotions were a mixed amazement and curiosity that one would come so close to my fire. My one cougar dog, Spot, had been sleeping under a shelter of boughs. Now she sat peering quizzically toward the sound. I threw back the big packsack which served as my only cover and reached for my boots. Again the heavy, guttural *m-e-e-o-w*

E. Boyd Hilderbrand in 1925 with cat he killed that year.

rasped the night. I've heard cougars scream only twice, but I've heard them meow many times, often when they were hunting together.

I slipped on the boots and lit my small miners' carbide lamp, my only source of light. The flickering glow was nearly useless in the snowstorm, but I walked toward the sound. I didn't have far to go. Within 30 feet of the fire, I found big pug marks. They were practically sizzling when touched by the wet snowflakes. I walked back to the fire and threw on a big supply of wood. Then I strapped on my 7.63 mm. Mauser pistol, a German weapon of World War I vintage with a combination holster and stock, and untied Spot. If this cougar was going to be brazen enough to wake me up, I was going after it. I estimated the time at about 11 p.m. If the cat pulled out and the snowstorm continued, I might not find its tracks by morning. I didn't have any idea how I would handle the situation if and when I treed the cat. I only knew that I had climbed nearly 15 miles up the side of a ridge looking for cat tracks. I wasn't going to pass up an opportunity like this, no matter what I might run up against.

It gave me a lot of satisfaction to hunt these cats. I had hunted and trapped coyotes professionally for years, but paid little attention to cougars. Then on December 17, 1924, James Fahlhaber, a 14-year-old orphan boy living with one of our neighbors, was killed by a cougar. At the time, I was living on my mother's homestead in the Chiliwist Basin about four miles southwest of Malott, Washington. Jimmie, who lived with the Robert L. Nash family on an adjoining homestead, started on foot through a canyon to get a team of mules from a neighboring homesteader. He never arrived. I was one of the first to reach the grisly scene of his death. What I saw left me with an unquenched hatred for cougars and started me on a lifelong onslaught on all members of the breed.

So far as I know, this was one of the few authenticated cases of a cougar making an unprovoked attack on a human. I might eventually have become reconciliated to this one case, but the hundreds of battered deer carcasses I have seen while following cougars have only heightened my hatred for them. I got Stub and Spot the same winter Jimmie was killed, and I declared war on cougars. I killed nearly 40 in the next three years, and earned such a reputation as a cat hunter that in 1929 I received the invitation to hunt them in Canada.

I had bedded down about 7 p.m. on a high ridge between Adams and Barriere Lakes in south-central British Columbia. It was December 22, 1929. Five days before I had entered Canada from the United States with Vernon Bawlf, a cousin who died in 1961. I had brought Stub and Spot and enough provisions to stay about two months. The British Columbia Game Commission had asked me to hunt the cougars that were causing serious depredations to deer and moose herds near Adams Lake. They offered me a bounty of $40 for each cat. As an added bonus, they gave me permission to shoot one deer for meat for every 10 cats I bagged.

We set up a base camp at Squim Bay, or Agate Bay as it is now called, about 10 miles above the lower end of Adams Lake. There was very little snow, and I had taken several cat tracks only to lose them on open ground. I decided to go higher where there might be more snow, so on December 22 I headed for the high ridge north of the lake. Vern stayed behind to tend camp, since he had come along on this trip mostly for the outing and to trap and poison coyotes and wolves along Adams Lake. I took one dog, Spot, and left Stub in camp. With a two-months hunt in prospect, I didn't want to wear out both dogs. I crossed the top of the ridge before nightfall and camped in a sheltered creek basin about six miles below the top, near Barriere Lakes. Just before dark, I had found three freshly killed and partly eaten deer carcasses, all dragged together in a thick patch of timber. This was highly unusual, and I knew there were plenty of cats around.

I carried no bedding, and depended upon a pile of boughs for a mattress and my packsack for a cover. I also cut a huge pile of wood so I could keep a large fire going all night. I must have been so tired that I didn't wake up when the snowstorm started and my fire died down. If that cougar had kept quiet, I would have missed one of the most amazing and dangerous adventures I was to experience in over 30 years of trailing the big cats.

Spot had no idea what had made that cry. I had used her on many cougars, but she had never heard one call. She walked beside me completely unconcerned until that strong cat smell rolled into her nostrils. Then she threw back her head and let go with a bawl that shook snow from the trees for 10 yards in every direction. Then she was gone, her baying sound lost and lonely In the darkness.

When I think back now, it seems unrealistic to put a dog on a hot cougar track at night and in the middle of a snowstorm. But I was only 37 years old then and in the peak of physical condition. I've

E. BOYD HILDERBRAND, 71 YEARS OLD, OF MALOTT, WASHINGTON, HAS SPENT THE MAJOR PART OF HIS LIFE AS A BOUNTY HUNTER.

He served as Deputy Sheriff of Okanogan County in 1928, as Sheriff from 1934 to 1938, and as Chief Deputy in 1939 and 1940. From 1941 to 1946, he worked for Washington State Department of Game. The author's lifelong war against cougars began in 1924, when he was one of the first to reach the death scene of James Fahlhaber, a 14-year-old boy killed by a cougar. Hilderbrand killed about 40 lions in the next three years.

Recent picture of author with his cougar gun

trailed cats under many adverse conditions, but never anything like that night. I couldn't see more than two or three yards ahead, and the snow was falling so fast it was covering Spot's tracks almost as fast as she made them. I could barely make out the big, round depressions in the snow where the cat had walked away from the fire. The cougar must have been too surprised to run.

Within three minutes, I could hear Spot telling me she had a cougar up a tree. I did the best I could, floundering along through the brush, practically feeling my way with Spot's bark as my only landmark. I found her at the base of a big fir. I tried to shine the little light up into the branches, but it was useless. Then I got an idea. A big snag had broken down about 20 yards away. The six-foot stump was hard and covered with pitch. In about 20 minutes I had the world's biggest candle lighting the whole area.

I looked up into the tree and finally made out two big glowing eyes. It was more than eerie with that stump thundering flame, great snowflakes flowing through the wavering light, and those big yellow spots suspended in the depths of the tree.

I fiitted the Mauser to the stock, aimed toward the eyes, and squeezed off five fast shots. The cat tumbled out of the tree and lay where it hit. After carefully keeping my distance for a few minutes, I walked up and nudged it with my foot. One of the slugs had found a fatal spot. The cat was a big female about five years old. Several of my bullets had hit her in the neck and chest.

It seemed to be snowing even harder, and I had no idea where my camp was. I knew the only way I was going to find it was to back-track if I could. I dragged the cougar under a tree where I hoped I might find it the next day, untied Spot, and started following the snow-filled impressions which I hoped were the tracks I'd made coming to the cat.

I hadn't gone more than 50 yards from the burning stump when Spot started acting up. I lowered the carbide lamp and took a better look at my tracks. Instead of oblong impressions under the new-fallen snow, there were clearcut, round impressions blotting them out. Another cougar had followed me right up to within 50 yards of the treed cat. I had often encountered cougars traveling together, so it didn't seem too unusual to find this second track. My only problem was that if I didn't find my camp before too much longer I might not find it at all.

Spot soon made up my mind for me. She began lunging and growl-ing, and I could tell from her actions that the cougar was right in

Hilderbrand shoulders one of the three cats he collected in Kamloops. B.C., in 1952.

front of us. This was more than I had bargained for, but I let her go. Apparently she was almost snapping at the cat's tail because within 250 yards the cougar treed.

Once again I found myself practically feeling my way through the night guided only by Spot's bark. This time I found her leaping at the base of a bushy fir tree. I walked up and pushed the carbide light through the branches.

It had climbed just high enough to avoid Spot's snapping teeth and there it sat, a great tawny blob in the feeble light with eyes glowing like two yellow coals. I checked the Mauser to make sure it was loaded. Then, holding the pistol in one hand and the light in the other, I lined up the sights on the cat. Had I known then what a chance I was taking I wouldn't have been so bold, but I'd never had a treed cougar even act as though it might jump me. I squeezed off three fast shots and stepped back. The cat thrashed around in the tree a few minutes and then fell to the ground, dead.

I looked over the second cougar and found it to be a large male. He apparently had been running with the female. Judging from the color and length of the hair and the condition of the teeth, the cat was about five years old. A cougar seems to grow slowly through most of its life. Its hair gradually becomes shorter and a grayness develops around the head and neck. The teeth are the best indicators of age; they become badly worn and are often cracked and broken in a very old tom.

The snow hadn't let up, and I still wanted to find camp. I was dragging this cat under another fir tree when I heard Spot bellow. I hadn't realized she was gone, and it was even harder to believe that she was on the trail of a third cougar. This was a lot more than I had expected. I was getting wet and   completely lost and had no idea where camp was or where I was. I had two dead cougars which I wasn't sure I would ever find again, and now my dog was trailing a third. Little did I know that I had just got through the best part of what was to be a long night.

Spot soon announced that she had done her job and was waiting for me to get there and polish off another pussycat. For the third time I groped along, trying to shield my face from limbs that seemed bent and cocked, ready to whip me as I passed. I floundered for at least half a mile to reach Spot's third victim. This cat was also just above the ground, and I could see it faintly with the carbide light. I aimed the pistol right between its eyes and squeezed the trigger. In an instant I knew I was in trouble. At the crack of the shot, one big yellow eye winked out. The cat jumped from the tree and was away in a flash.

For the next hour or so I went through one of the most nightmarish experiences of my entire hunting career. Spot would tree the wounded cat and I would go crashing toward her, raked by hidden limbs and tripped by hundreds of invisible snags. Then the cat would jump the tree when I approached and the whole thing would start over again.

Around and around and back and forth I slogged. I didn't know if I would ever find my camp and was reaching the point of not caring. I just lunged on with a fanatical determination to finish off that wounded cougar. Finally, the cat stayed treed on a small leaning tree trunk. He was perched about 10 feet from the ground, spitting and snarling at Spot. Under any other circumstances I would have been far more cautious, knowing that a wounded cougar could easily prove dangerous. But I was too tired and exhausted to care.

I walked right up under the cat, shoved the pistol under its chin, and put a bullet through and out the top of its head. It was another big male, about six years old. My first shot had hit him squarely in the eye. The bullet had been deflected by the hard, bony shell around his brain, and had gone right on through and out the side of his head.

Nearing exhaustion, I knew I had to get back to camp and get dried out and some grub in me as soon as possible. From my memory of the lay of the land, I knew I was on the opposite side of the basin from camp. I threw the cat under a tree and started off in the direction I hoped might lead me to my campfire. Spot followed behind me.

Without her barking, the night would have been a complete void. I could have been on a wet, cold, lightless planet. My world was wrapped around me in the faint, flickering circle of light cast by the carbide. By an amazing streak of good luck, I hit some of the tracks I made earlier in the evening and somehow found my way to camp.

Sometime during my wanderings, Spot disappeared. If I hadn't been so miserable, I would have been sure I was dreaming when I heard her sound off on another hot track. Somewhere she had found the tracks of a fourth cougar. By this time I didn't care if she treed that cat on my shoulder. I just kept going until I found camp. I built up a big fire, dried my clothing the best I could, and ate some food. Spot had treed her fourth cougar about a mile up the canyon. I could hear her faint tree bark bucking the sodden darkness. I could visualize her, leaping and yapping at the base of a tree, pleased with herself for such an outstanding performance. I hated to fail her, but I just didn't have the strength to get there.

The snowstorm never let up. I got as dry as possible, brushed the snow away from my bough bed, and lay down, getting as much cover as I could from my packsack. I was so tired I could have slept hanging over a tree limb. It must have been about 9 o'clock when I finally woke up. My fire had died and I had nearly 10 inches of wet snow piled on top of me. If it had been cold I would have nearly frozen to death. But all that snow on top of my heavy wool clothing had provided a lot of warmth. Spot had finally given up and come back.

After a big breakfast, I went in search of my three cougars. It had snowed nearly 16 inches in all, and I could find absolutely no trace of my tracks made during the nightmarish chase.

I had nearly given up when I hit a fresh cat track. I was almost certain it had been made by the fourth cougar searching for its companions. I decided to follow.

Before the day was over, I was to undergo a second experience that stands out as one of the most unusual during a lifetime of cougar hunting. That cat had searched until it found each of its three dead companions. Then it had pawed the snow away from their bodies and had lain on top of the carcasses.

I had only to follow the wandering tracks until all three dead cougars had been located. I have no explanation for this other than that the cat was lonely and confused by the sudden disappearance of its comrades.

I spent the entire day skinning the three cats and packing the hides and my grub back to a campsite at the top of the ridge in an old burn. It was nearly six miles but I took the whole works in one load, making it just before dark. I hung two of the skins on a low snag and used the third for a bed.

I slept long and well that night. I awoke early and got up with the intention of going back down the mountain to see if I might still find the fourth cougar. It had snowed about half an inch during the night, and I knew I wouldn't have any trouble picking up the freshest tracks if the cougar was still there. I ate a huge breakfast and loaded enough grub in my packsack for another meal. Then I started back down the mountain.

I hadn't walked more than 40 yards when I came to a big burned log lying flat on the ground. There, in a straight line leading out across the top of the ridge, were a set of pug marks on top of the fresh snow. The cat had followed me to the top of the mountain and had slept alongside the log all night. I am sure it had watched me for a while at daylight, and then walked away in plain sight without my noticing it.

I'm certain none of these cougars had ever seen man or dog and had absolutely no fear of us. It was only Spot's baying that put them to rout when I set her on their tracks. The fourth cat had gone north until it reached a strip of green timber about 50 yards wide. This timber followed a shallow draw and had somehow escaped the old forest fire. The cougar had walked to the edge and had then turned downhill following parallel with the near side.

I had just tracked it to the point where it turned when I heard a terrific commotion below me and across the draw. There were sounds of limbs cracking and then a sound as though someone were beating dried brush to pieces with a heavy club. I sneaked along, following the tracks about 200 yards.

The cat had turned down into the draw. The green trees were heavily loaded with wet snow, and the cougar had crossed through them and out into the burn on the other side. It had circled a small knoll and had crept to within 50 yards of a five-point mule deer that was eating some green alders. The buck had been facing downhill, and the cat had taken about five long jumps and landed squarely on his back, knocking him down. The noise I had heard had been the buck kicking and thrashing in the alders while the cougar held him by the back of the neck.

The cat had then dragged the buck back through the burn and down into the strip of green timber. I'm sure it let me approach to within 50 yards before it deserted the buck and walked into the brush. This was the first and last time I was ever within hearing distance of a cougar making a kill, but there was one thing about it that intrigued me even more.

In preparing to eat some of the buck, the cat had completely sheared a 16-inch circle of hair away from the left side of the carcass. The hair had been clipped as neatly and as closely as any pair of barber shears could have done. In addition, the cat had piled the hair in a nice little stack off to one side. A cougar's front teeth match perfectly and the edges are razor sharp. Apparently, it had nipped this hair away in little tufts with those sharp clippers. I followed the tracks a short distance to get Spot away from the deer, and then I set her on the track.

I didn't want to fight my way through the snow-laden trees, so I crossed the draw and had just reached the burned area when I heard Spot bark treed. I followed along the green timber for about a quarter of a mile until I reached a position opposite her homing signal coming from the draw.

There was the cougar standing on a leaning windfall some 15 feet above the ground. Although it was about 60 yards away, I decided to take a shot from where I was since I was afraid it might jump if I tried to get to a point under it.

I put the Mauser pistol on the stock and took careful aim. When the shot cracked I saw the hair puff on the cat's ribs, but a little too far back. In an instant the cat was gone, and I could only follow the bellowing chase with my ears.

In about 60 yards Spot treed again. Once more the cat had climbed up a low, slanting windfall, and I knew when I walked up to the scene that I had a very angry female cougar to contend with. She was only about 10 feet from the ground, and a picture of absolute rage—eyes glowing, ears laid flat, lips rolled back from long, polished teeth.

Spot was doing her best to get a chunk of cougar between her teeth, and the cat was spitting vehemently, while taking vicious uppercuts in her direction. I walked up to within 15 feet and drew the handgun out of the holster, raising it at arms length with the barrel almost straight up.

In that instant, fate decided to throw in the final chilling touch to my greatest cougar-hunting adventure. A huge mass of wet snow dropped from directly above me and landed squarely on the upended barrel. I should have known better than to take my eyes from the cat, but I never thought she might jump me. I reached down, broke off a small twig, and inserted it into the pistol barrel. I was working out the snow when a sudden movement caught my eye and caused me to look up. The cougar had crouched and was already in the middle of an open-jawed, death-dealing spring.

She came sailing at me as if she'd been shot from a circus cannon—a heart-stopping vision of hate-filled eyes, white teeth, and hook-rimmed paws. In one instinctive lunge, I threw myself down and to one side. The cat sailed by, practically combing my whiskers with a vicious hooking swipe as she passed. If she'd ever landed on bare ground I wouldn't be telling this story. But when she hit that deep, wet snow and tried to turn, she momentarily lost her footing. In the extra second it took her to get her feet gathered, I had time to half roll and twist to face her charge.

There was no time to worry about snow in the barrel. I thrust the pistol in her face and felt, more than heard, the staccato hammering as I ran a full magazine of slugs into her oncoming head and body. She died in midstride, falling within inches of my outstretched leg.

It would be foolish to say I wasn't scared, but at a time like that the will to survive overcomes all fear. I was completely aware that I had come within a hairbreadth of vanishing in the Canadian wilds. Apparently, all the indignities I had inflicted upon this cougar were just too much. I had set my dog on her, killed her companions, taken a deer away from her, and then followed all this up by wounding her. Though I killed 10 more cougars on that one trip, and dozens more in the next 28 years, I never again had a cougar try to jump me.

I loaded the four skins and packed them down to Adams Lake that same day. It wasn't until I reached the ranch of a family named Todd that I realized it was Christmas Eve. I spent the night there and returned to my own camp to join Vern on Christmas Day.

I still hunt a lot, but I haven't hunted the big cats since 1957. It must have been one more quirk of fate to decree that I should get my last two near the head of Adams Lake that year when I was 65 years old. If I never take the trails again, I have a lot of thrilling memories, and this great experience sits right at the top.

Outdoor Life, July 1963

Man-Eaters of the Iron Snake

BY BRIAN HERNE

In 1896, construction began on Kenya's Uganda Railway, or Iron Snake, as it was called by African tribesmen. More than 32,000 workers were brought in for the task; the local lions were there to take the laborers out.

Mrs. O'Hara awoke to the sound of her baby, who lay restless and feverish in the hot African night.

The older child in the same bed seemed to be sleeping comfortably, but the infant needed water. As she got up, Mrs. O'Hara heard something and shook her husband. "Wake up," she whispered. "I think there's a lion outside the tent."

O'Hara jumped up, grabbed his gun, and stepped out for a look. Nothing. He called to question the Swahili askari (soldier) who was on sentry duty beside a nearby fire. "No simba, B'wana," was the answer. "Only donkey."

O'Hara threw back the tent flap to relieve the stifling heat and returned to his wife's bed. "Nothing to worry about," he assured her. "Only a donkey."

Mrs. O'Hara eventually dozed off, but was suddenly awakened by something dragging across her pillow and pulling it from under her head. Terrified to see that she was alone, Mrs. O'Hara jumped up and screamed for her husband. There was no answer, but she heard a noise among the boxes outside the tent. She ran through the tent flaps, and to her horror found Mr. O'Hara sprawled between the boxes. "Come help me!" she yelled to the askari.

He refused, terror in his voice. "Simba stand by you!"

Mrs. O'Hara looked up and saw the man-eating lion glowering at her from barely two yards away. The askari fired his rifle at that moment, and the lion, fortunately too inexperienced at its grizzly occupation to be totally scornful of unfamiliar human noises, leaped away into the bush.

Four soldiers then rushed to Mrs. O'Hara's aid, but it was too late. The lion's fangs had entered her husband's temples to meet in his brain. Death had been instantaneous.

The beast's fear of the rifle was shortlived, however. Almost as soon as the body was dragged into the tent, the huge cat was back, pacing in front of the door, threatening to reclaim its prey. The soldiers fired and frightened it away again, but only for a moment. The lion prowled around the tent until daylight, kept out only by Mrs. O'Hara and the soldiers occasionally firing through the tent at the sounds outside.

History does not even leave us with Mr. O'Hara's first name, perhaps because in the turn-of-the-century Victorian manners of the British, first names were used only in the most intimate of friendships. More ominously, perhaps it was because the killing of one more human by a lion was not an event noteworthy enough to record a first name. This was 1899, and the place was 12 miles out of Voi, which

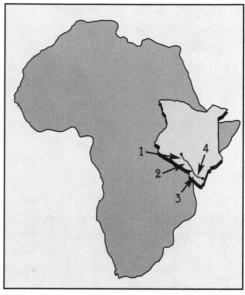

The Iron Snake—today's Kenya Railway—stretches from Mombasa on the coast northwest to Nairobi and beyond. Lion attacks were reported up and down the line. Some of the notable stations that are mentioned in the story include 1) Voi, 2) Tsavo, 3) Kima and 4) Kiu.

is about 100 miles from Mombasa on the Kenya coast. Work had begun on the Uganda Railway in 1896, and lions along the way had come to regard the 32,000 imported Indian workers plus Europeans and nearby Africans as just another herd of prey animals to feed upon. O'Hara had been an engineer in charge of road building.

My grandfather, David Edward Herne, a surveyor, walked ahead of the railway construction from Mombasa to Nairobi (a city of three tents when he was there) and then on into Uganda and Lake Victoria at the head of the Nile River. The Uganda Railway, later renamed East African Railways and Harbours, and now known as Kenya Railways, was called the Iron Snake by African tribesmen. It was no surprise to them when a lion began man-eating at one camp or another along the Snake. They assumed that it was always a powerful dead chief returning in the form of a lion to punish those who would cut the ugly gash through the land.

Back in England, the railway was called the Lunatic Line by members of Parliament who thought it insane to spend $8 million building a rail more than 600 miles long through sometimes nearly impassable terrain into a useless wilderness. More powerful members of Parliament pushed the railway through, convinced that they needed to protect the headwaters of the Nile from the territorially minded Germans.

But the average British citizen heard much more about the line's noble purpose of gaining access far enough inland to combat the Arab slavers who ran caravans from Africa's coast all the way to the Congo River. By 1909, however, the year my granduncle, Billy Judd, accompanied Teddy Roosevelt on safari, the slavers were finished. Sultan Ali bin Hamoud of Zanzibar, an island off Tanzania, had decreed the emancipation of all slaves.

If history treated O'Hara badly, it was less kind to the "nameless" Wataita tribesman who, a few weeks later, killed the man-eating lion with a poison arrow. Although he made his shot from the safety of a tree, the tribesman's courage was enormous because he probably believed that he was killing the instrument of a spirit demon who would seek revenge.

About every 30 miles along the railway, a station was built of concrete block with a corrugated sheet metal roof. The "platform" beside each was simply a leveled patch of ground. Also at each was a large tank standing on tall legs to supply the steam locomotives with water. The names of some of the stations were grotesquely accurate: Tsavo (slaughter), Simba (lion) and Kima (mincemeat).

Railway construction reached Tsavo, 130 miles inland from Mombasa, in the second year. Except during the brief, lush growth after the April/May rains, the whole country around Tsavo seems slaughtered. The earth is bright red, as if soaked in blood. Quartz rock litters the kopjes, or hills. Scattered acacia trees appear flat-topped, the multi-trunks with the leaves at the tops giving the impression of hands, raised palms up, beseeching the heavens for rain. Between the trees are leafless, bleached-bone-whitish thornbush. Lions here have scraggly manes, as lots of hair remains behind on thornbush when the big cats pass through. Open areas are short-grass savannas, dead yellow in color for most of the year. And through this water-starved area, the Galana River flows year-round as a reminder of the unexpected that is Africa.

It was at Tsavo that two lions brought the entire railway to a halt. Col. J. H. Patterson, a construction engineer, had barely arrived at the station when the killings began. At first, the stories of Indian coolies (laborers) carried off at night weren't believed. Some workers had saved their rupees, and murder for money was suspected. Not even the Indians were terribly concerned. There were always 2,000 to 3,000 coolies in the railhead camp, so individuals saw their odds of survival as quite good. When the main camp moved on, leaving just a few hundred to complete the permanent works, fear escalated along with the odds of being selected by lions.

Patterson believed the lion stories when Ungan Singh, one of his jemandars (Indian army officers) was dragged from a tent of seven men. "Chora!" (let go) the officer yelled, and threw his arms around the lion's neck as they left the tent. Ungan Singh was a powerful man and died hard, but the remaining six men were helpless to do anything but listen to the struggle. Patterson followed the lion's tracks and found his jemandar's remains: scattered bits of blood and flesh and the officer's head with eyes open in a startled, horrified look. Lions often begin feeding on the extremities of their kills and work toward the head. Evidence indicated that two lions had shared the meal.

The same two lions continued to share one another's kills. Bomas (thorn fences) were piled around the scattered camps in attempts to keep out the man-eaters. Fires were kept blazing at night. Empty oil tins were clattered all night long by the watchmen. Ever braver, the lions found thin, low or weak spots where they could jump over or push through the bomas. One of the man-eaters jumped over a new fence, stuck its head under the canvas wall of a tent, and grabbed a hospital bhisti (water carrier) by a foot. The desperate man clung to a heavy box, which was wrenched from his grip by the tent wall as he was dragged past it, then seized a tent rope until it broke, leaving him to be clenched by the throat and dragged through a boma. Torn cloth, blood and bits of flesh marked the path through the thorns.

Col. Patterson was inexperienced at hunting, but he was very courageous. Night after night he took a position near an attack site or where the remains of a kill had been left by a lion, expecting the man-eaters to return. Unfortunately, his presence and his missed shots only taught the man-eaters never to return to either. Each time hunger demanded a new victim, the lions chose a different camp. Sometimes Patterson was near enough to hear the victims' helpless screams. Once he was in a goods wagon with the camp doctor. Both heard the lion jump over the boma; both fancied that they saw the man-eater move in the darkness; but neither shot until the lion actually sprang at them. The double flash perhaps blinded the lion, and it missed its mark and disappeared. Neither bullet found its mark, either. Eventually, the lions concluded that gunfire was harmless fireworks. The man-eaters attacked within a stone's throw of Tsavo Station during the night, and calmly finished their meal while more than 50 shots were fired in their direction.

Unable to do more than educate lions with his firearms, Patterson built a two-section trap of railroad ties, iron rails, chain and telegraph wire. Into one section went the bait: Patterson himself. That lasted only a few nights, however, as the lions moved to the railhead to kill five more people there and along the way. When they returned to snatch a sleeping worker and go no farther than over the boma to eat him— despite gunfire from a jemandar—the trap was once again baited, this time by two Indian soldiers armed with Martini rifles.

About 9 P.M. the trap door clattered down. Everyone waited for gunfire. Nothing. The soldiers were frozen with fear. Someone yelled a command to shoot. They did, in whatever directions their guns were pointed. Although the rifle muzzles literally could have been stuck in the lion's ear, none of the bullets touched the man-eater. The soldiers did succeed in blowing out a bar in the door, however, and the lion escaped.

By this time, the Indians were in such a state of terror that work had completely stopped. They informed Patterson that they had not signed on as food for lions. Hundreds stopped the first train by throwing themselves on the rails, then clambered aboard. For three weeks, the brave ones who stayed did nothing but build beds and shelters above ground on bridge girders, roofs, water tanks and in trees. One night during an attack, so many coolies swarmed a single tree that it crashed to the ground, throwing them at the man-eaters they sought to escape. The lions, already busy eating a victim, ignored the commotion.

In all, 28 Indian workers were killed, and nobody knew how many Africans were eaten in the nearby bush. Finally, about nine months after the man-eating had started, a Swahili came running toward Patterson shouting "Simba! Simba!" The lion had tried to kill an African, but had missed and gotten a donkey instead. Patterson grabbed a large-caliber double rifle that had been left by the superintendent of police, and without test-firing a single cartridge, sneaked into the dense bush to catch the lion on its kill. The beast heard a twig snap and disappeared into an even more dense patch of thorn.

Patterson then coerced his workers to half-circle the patch and advance while beating cans and tom-toms to frighten the man-eater toward him. It worked! The huge maneless lion stepped out onto the path where Patterson stood, frequently looking back and not noticing the engineer with the untried rifle.

When the rifle came up, the surprised lion caught the motion and dropped to its haunches, growling menacingly. The sights covered the cat's brain, Patterson pulled, and . . . snap. The cartridge misfired. Nervous about the din behind it, the lion leaped into the bush, just as Patterson remembered to try the other barrel. He thought the lion was hit, but it escaped.

Forsaking the borrowed rifle in favor of his .303 British, Patterson then built a flimsy 12-foot-high platform about 10 feet from the dead donkey. It was simply four poles angled toward each other at the top, where a plank was tied as a seat. Darkness closed around Patterson with an extraordinary stillness, perhaps because something was lurking near enough to inhibit the usual makers of noise in the night. Finally, a twig snapped. A deep, long-drawn sigh signaled the lion's hunger. But it didn't want the donkey. For two hours it crept in circles around the structure, slowly spiraling closer and closer as it tried to pinpoint its prey.

Suddenly, Patterson realized both how flimsy his platform was and that 12 feet was not too high for the lion to jump. By midnight, he was so strained that he could scarcely blink his eyes, when whap! Something struck the back of his head. Certain that it was the lion, Patterson yelped involuntarily. But the lion growled back from below. An owl had mistaken Patterson for a tree, or perhaps his head for something edible.

Again, the lion crept closer. Patterson could barely see a dark form against the whitish thornbush. Taking careful aim, he fired, and continued firing at the sound of the lunging, plunging lion. At last a mankiller was dead. The Indians prostrated before Patterson, crying, "Mabarah! Mabarah!" which the astonished engineer believed to mean "savior." The Swahilis and other Africans spent the balance of the night in an especially wild dance.

A few nights later, the second lion was back prowling on the veranda of the Permanent Way Inspector's bungalow. Unable to get inside, the man-eater settled for a pair of goats.

The next night, Patterson waited nearby in a sheet metal shanty. Three goats were tied to a 250-pound half-length rail. The lion obliged, but again Patterson had no flashlight, the night was black, and he could only fire at the sounds. The man-eater grabbed one goat and dragged off the other two with it, rail and all.

In the morning, the drag trail was easily followed a quarter-mile to dense brush, where a threatening growl revealed a lion's presence. The man-eater made a defensive charge, sending Patterson's assistants into trees, but then ducked away into thornbush before a shot could be fired.

Because the two other goats had remained uneaten, Patterson had a *strong* scaffold built nearby. That night, he and Mahina, his gun bearer, took turns watching. Just as Patterson dozed, Mahina grabbed his arm and pointed. Bushes rustled, the lion emerged, and Patterson fired both slugs from his smoothbore double as the man-eater stalked directly beneath him. The beast went down for an instant, then disappeared.

In daylight, the blood trail was easily followed for more than a mile. The lion had paused several times as if severely wounded. But then the trail ended on rocky ground. Cautious hope that the lion was dead lasted just 10 days when trolley men, sleeping in a tree outside Patterson's boma, began yelling that a lion was circling them. Patterson could only fire aimlessly into the total darkness of the cloudy night, but the lion left.

The next night, Patterson and Mahina waited in the tree. About 3 A.M. Patterson thought he saw a movement, continued to watch the spot, and saw the lion emerge, stalking them, taking advantage of the few small bushes in its effort to remain concealed. At 20 yards, Patterson fired his .303 into the man-eater's chest, but instead of going down, the lion growled and bounded off amid three more shots. One of the shots drew another growl.

Again waiting for daylight, Patterson had an African tracker do the trailing so that he could be more alert for a sudden charge. The blood trail was easily followed for a quarter-mile, whereupon a threatening growl warned "come no farther." Looking carefully into the bushes, Patterson could see the lion, teeth bared in a snarl. He fired, and the man-eater charged. He fired again, knocking the animal down with a broken hind leg, but instantly the lion was back up—slowed, but coming. His rifle empty, Patterson reached behind him for the Martini carbine, only to learn that his gun bearer and the carbine were already up a tree. Patterson followed just in time to escape the lion's reach.

Grabbing the carbine from Mahina, Patterson shot again, rolling the lion. With an amateur's talent for doing the wrong thing, Patterson clambered down and confidently walked toward the man-eater. But the lion again jumped up to charge, falling five feet from Patterson after one more shot to the chest. Six bullet holes were in the body.

One slug from the smoothbore had penetrated little farther than the skin on the lion's back.

News traveled quickly, and Africans came from up and down the line to see the "devil killer" and his trophies. The coolies who had been determined to return to India flocked back to work at Tsavo.

J. A. Hunter, a Kenya pioneer and close friend of my family, has a theory about those man-eaters. Hunter went to Africa just after the railway was finished, was a game warden most of his life, and dealt with a large number of man-eaters himself. A wonderful man, he took me hunting as a boy, and we had many memorable conversations. The railway had cost the lives of 2,500 men through injury, disease and man-eating lions. "Brian," Hunter explained, "when those men died, unarmed parties of coolies were sent out in the bush to bury the dead. Often, those frightened coolies simply dumped the bodies and ran, leaving easy meals that introduced the lions to man-eating."

As the Iron Snake crawled on toward Nairobi, the landscape changed. The strange baobabs, with the huge trunks and horizontal branches that make them appear to be upside down, became fewer and disappeared altogether as the countryside became more and more arid. The bushes changed to whistling thorn, never more than six feet high, and only patches existed here and there on the short-grass plains. The herds of savanna animals—zebras, wildebeests and gazelles—were abundant, but they did not curb the appetites that certain lions had for human flesh.

Shortly after the railhead had reached Nairobi, a lion at Kima, just 69 miles back down the tracks, had become so bold that it climbed onto the roof of the station building and tried to break through the corrugated sheet metal to get at the station master inside. The terrified Indian telegraphed to the traffic manager at Nairobi: "Lion fighting with station. Send urgent succour."

Help did not arrive promptly, but the lion failed to gain entrance. It cut its paws, tracked blood about the roof, then left. Soon after, however, the lion carried off an African pumping-engine driver. The man-eater had already claimed several African gangers who had been building the crushed-rock railway bed and laying the sleepers, or ties. An Indian pointsman (switchman) had been eaten, too. The Wakamba tribesmen of the area were terrorized, and the station's staff, safer because they were inside houses, would not venture outside from sunset to sunrise.

Several European railway officials hunted the Kima killer unsuccessfully. A "nameless" engine driver cut an entry hole in a large galvanized water tank lying on the station platform and crawled inside with his rifle to plan an ambush. The Kima lion obliged him in the middle of the night by tipping the tank on its side and reaching into the hole with a front leg in an effort to hook the man out of his hiding place. The driver could only cower against the opposite side of the tank to avoid the claws. Eventually, the lion withdrew to plan a different strategy, and the man frightened it off with random gunfire out of the port.

Finally, Superintendent Charles Ryall, of the Railway Police at Mombasa, was going to Nairobi on official business and decided to lay over in Kima for an attempt at the man-eater. Ryall, who had shikaried (the Indian version of safaried) during his service in India and who had hunted in Kenya since his arrival, thought he had a great idea. Trader/Mombasa Italian Vice Consul Parenti and a German merchant named Huebner had been refused permission to ride the construction train and tried to hitch a ride with Ryall. He explained his plan. If they agreed to stand watch for the lion, they would be given berths. Parenti was anxious to do business in Nairobi. Huebner intended to go beyond the railhead into Uganda on foot. Both eagerly agreed. Another policeman, Inspector Bishen Singh, joined the party to investigate thefts from the staff at Kiu (which means thirst) Station, 30 miles past Kima to the west.

When the train made the stop at Kima before traveling on to Kiu, Ryall had his white inspection coach switched onto the side track, about 20 yards from the station building. It was a composite coach with a door in each end. Two living compartments were separated by a hall leading past a small toilet compartment. Ryall's Indian cook and a bearer slept in one compartment, which they also used as a kitchen. Ryall occupied the other compartment with his partners. They drew for watches, intending to ambush the man-eater from the safety of the coach.

Parenti drew the dusk-to-midnight shift and spent his watch near the open door. Huebner, although a large man, climbed onto the top bunk, courteously leaving the lower bunk to Ryall. Huebner's was to be the 3 A.M.-to-dawn watch. According to the attentive Indian station master, talking ceased and lights went out at 10 P.M.

Parenti woke Ryall at midnight and rolled himself in a blanket on the floor beside the lower bunk. Ryall opened the three windows above his bunk, then sat back down with a rifle across his lap, propping himself with pillows to watch the open door from the comfort of his bed. Parenti heard Ryall comment that he could see the eyes of two rats "shining like lamps" in the darkness outside, then Parenti fell asleep.

Apparently, Ryall also dozed off. And apparently both eyes belonged to the Kima lion, which stood outside staring intently at Ryall's silhouette against the windows. When all was silent, the man-eater stepped up the footboard, mounted the platform, then stalked through the open sliding door.

Parenti's eyes flew open to the stench of the man-eater's breath and the horribly awakening realization that the lion was standing on his chest. He tried to squirm from under the lion, but the weight pinned him helplessly to the floor. The beast growled savagely, and Parenti thought the end had come, but the man-eater had stepped on him to reach Ryall, its intended victim. Before the growl ended, the huge cat's jaws had gripped Ryall by the neck. The man never uttered a sound.

Huebner, brought sharply awake by the growl, panicked. He rolled off the bunk, fell heavily on the lion's back, dropped to the floor, raced to the toilet, and locked the door behind him.

The lion turned to exit with his victim, and found itself trapped. Owing to poorly laid sleepers, the coach stood slightly tilted on its rails. The commotion of heavy bodies had disturbed the delicately balanced, wheel-mounted door, which had slid shut and latched.

With Ryall still in its jaws, the man-eater turned to the open central window and tried to get out. That the lion struggled at length was evident from the splintered condition of the window frame. The man-eater was a sitting shot the whole time, and Parenti's rifle lay beside him, but the trader was too unnerved to move.

Once the lion was gone, Parenti scrambled from a window on the opposite side of the coach and ran to the station building, where doors were not opened at night for any reason. Finally, hearing enough of the frantic man's story, the station master let Parenti in and telegraphed Kiu Station for help.

Trains were not yet authorized to run at night, but the locomotive stabled for the night at Kiu left for Kima almost immediately. Aboard were a guard named Howard, section engineer Smith, Mombasa postmaster-general Remington and Inspector Bishen Singh.

They found only panic and confusion when they arrived at Kima shortly before dawn, and nothing had been done to recover Ryall's body. Smith assumed command and called for volunteers. Huebner and Parenti refused. Remington tried to pull rank, insisting that he had "urgent business" and that the train should take him on to Mombasa immediately. Smith detailed Howard to see that the train did not move.

Smith carried a heavy rifle. Inspector Bishen Singh had just his revolver and a sword. The only other volunteers were Ryall's two loyal Indian servants. The bearer carried his master's rifle, which he had never fired, and the cook bravely went forth with the others at dawn, carrying nothing but a meat cleaver.

Fifteen minutes later, Howard heard two rapidly fired shots signaling that Ryall's remains had been found. Almost certainly, the lion had been near its kill, but it had slipped away at the sounds of men and guns. There was no tracker in the group, so the man-eater was not pursued any farther.

Another colony pioneer, a member of the Kenya police, and a good friend of my family, was W. Robert Foran, who investigated the incident thoroughly. During one of our many long conversations, Foran told me in an almost police-report manner and detail that Ryall's body was found beneath a small bush, barely eaten despite the hours that the man-eater had had it in its possession. Ryall had been disemboweled, and his intestines had been dragged off a short distance. His throat was badly lacerated, but only one thigh had been eaten. Ryall's remains were buried at the foot of Nairobi's Railway Hill. The granite gravestone reads: "He was attacked whilst sleeping and killed by a man-eating lion at Kima." Other graves have since appeared, bearing the simple epitaph: "Killed by a Lion."

Chief railway engineer Sir George Whitehouse offered a reward of 100 pounds for the man-eater, plus 15 pounds for every lion killed between Makindu Station and Nairobi, a distance of 119 miles. Ryall's stricken mother offered another 100 pounds for the killer, dead or alive.

Many lions were shot on the designated stretch of line over the next few weeks, five of them near Kima Station. The lion killed closest to the station was one of 12 taken by engine driver W. Dennett. All were claimed to be the Kima lion, of course, but all were denied the 200 pounds reward because, it was said, "a man-eater's stench proclaims it for what it is, so there is little room for error." Indeed, man-eating continued.

A locomotive foreman named Costello and a switchman named Rodrigues tried a different approach. They built a sturdy drop-door trap about a mile from Kima and baited it with a live calf. The trap was sprung the first day. Delighted, they hurried to the trap, only to find two young Wakamba boys inside. Sending the admonished would-be calf stealers on their way, the partners fed the calf and reset the trap. For two months, the partners fed and watered the calf while the man-eater continued to kill African and Indian workers.

Finally, their patience was rewarded by a very angry lion behind bars. The beast was viewed and photographed for several days, then shot. Man-eating in that area ended, and eventually Sir George Whitehouse conceded that the Kima killer had been caught. Costello and Rodrigues received Whitehouse's reward, but for some reason, Dennett, who had killed a dozen lions but not the man-eater, shared in Mrs. Ryall's 100 pounds. The infamous coach is still on display at Nairobi's Railway Museum.

The fine condition of the heavily maned Kima lion reminds me again of J. A. Hunter's theory that not burying victims had sometimes initiated man-eating along the railway. We normally think that man-eaters should be too old, too sick, too toothless, or too crippled to kill more difficult game. That is not always the case, no matter where man-eating occurs, as the numbers of perfectly healthy man-eaters along the railway attest.

I recall another point that Hunter made. "Once a lion kills a person, it acquires a taste for the saltier blood and flesh of human beings." Perhaps Hunter was right. He was widely experienced, and he had safaried across eastern Africa and all of the way into cannibal country of the Congo. I have often wondered who told him, or how he learned, that human flesh is salty. He would never say.

Outdoor Life, April 1990

Varmint Calling Can Be Dangerous to Your Health

by Reed Peterson

"Every time I sit down to call now, I get an uneasy feeling," one varmint caller told me. You'd feel the same way if you had been clouted on the side of the head by a mountain lion.

The soft yucca leaves swayed gently in the cool fall breeze that was rapidly lulling me to sleep. The effects of driving all night from Mesa to that remote part of Arizona's Fort Apache Reservation was taking its toll.

Then a sudden gust of wind rattled the tall, dry century plant behind me, and the noise startled me. I again started to coax softly with my predator call. I had only called a few seconds when another wave of drowsiness engulfed me. I made up my mind that if a coyote or bobcat didn't respond in the next few minutes, I'd head for camp and some much-needed sleep.

As I let the call slip my from my mouth, I thought I heard a rock roll below me, slightly to my left. I was wide awake in an instant. Years of calling experience had taught me to look to the side without the slightest movement of my head. To my amazement, staring in my direction over a patch of prickly pear cactus at a distance of a little less than 50 yards, was a magnificent bear. His jet-black coat glistened in the sunlight and his great head swayed slightly from side to side as he surveyed the situation.

I could hardly keep from laughing out loud at the ridiculousness of the situation. My two hunting companions, Jim James and Lester Bradley, were somewhere up on the mountain a few thousand feet above me, trying to call in a bear. There I was down in prickly pear country near the floor of the desert with a bear practically in my lap. I hadn't the slightest interest in killing another bear, even though I had a permit in my possession and the Arizona bear season had been open for nearly a month. Through the years, I had exceptionally good luck at calling bears and with a couple of truly fine trophy blacks already mounted in my den, I had no desire to take another. I have been content for the last decade to call for friends who want to take a bear.

My inner laughter over the situation was extremely short-lived. The next 60 seconds or so completely changed my outlook on varmint calling.

The giant black reared up on his hind legs, searched intently for whatever was making the sound and then dropped back on all fours and methodically moved up the hill straight toward me. Again I chuckled to myself and decided to see how close I could call him in. Again, I started coaxing softly on the call. The bear was not in a hurry but plodded steadily uphill toward the spot where I sat concealed. He looked as big as a barn and I thought, "Man, most hunters would give their eyeteeth for a trophy like that."

At 25 yards it got a little spooky, and I decided he was close enough. I reached down and picked up a small rock. As I tossed it at him, I let out a *"Ya-a-ah"* that could have been heard a mile away. The rock sailed over the back of the animal. I was sure that yell would send the big bear crashing down the mountain in full flight, but he reared up again on his hind legs and let out a deep growl that chilled me.

"Perhaps he still doesn't know I'm a human," I thought, and I jerked my camouflage hat and veil off with one quick sweep of my hand and at the same time squalled *"Ya-a-ah,* get out of here!" at the top of my lungs. The great bear dropped back on all fours and with that same unhurried, swaying motion, continued toward me.

It was unreal. I leaped to my feet and with the bear only 15 yards away, I snatched up a rock the size of a grapefruit and let fly with all the force I could muster and screamed *"Ya-a-ah!"* once again. The rock sailed harmlessly over his head, and the bear didn't even pause.

I had heard all my life of the great speed of a charging bear, but the big boar never changed his methodical gait or took his eyes off me. Time seemed suspended and confused thoughts were running through my brain.

At 10 yards the great black snarled, his canine teeth gleaming in the sunlight. I swore softly and whipped my rifle to my shoulder. In that instant, a sickening thought struck me. My custom 7mm magnum was in my truck. All that stood between me and the bear was my .243 and 80-grain varmint loads.

I frantically tried to place the crosshairs on the great bear's head but at that range, all I could see through my 4X Redfield scope was hair. I was in serious trouble.

At seven yards, the black crashed through a small prickly pear patch, seemingly indifferent to the sharp spines. He was exactly 15 feet away when my finger closed on the trigger. The animal stopped as though hit by a cannon and let out a bawl of rage and pain. I ejected the spent case and put another round into the chamber so fast that I was scarcely conscious I had done so. I didn't pull the trigger the second time because the giant black sank slowly to the ground without another sound. Blood began to trickle from a small hole just left of center between the animal's eyes.

I stood there without moving a muscle, staring at the downed bear. I was in a trance for some time and I just continued to stare. Then my knees began to shake, so hard that I had to sit down.

A few years have elapsed since that morning, but I remember only too well my thoughts while I sat there shaking. Had the bullet hit the bear only a few inches from where it did, I would not have had time enough to fire a second shot.

I have been using a varmint call for nearly 25 years. Some say that it's an obsession. That is exaggerated, but I do believe varmint calling is the most fascinating form of hunting, and that big bear demonstrated that calling can be dangerous. Anyone who thinks otherwise is either a fool or hasn't spent enough time in the field. Novice callers should be aware of the danger.

The number of attacks on callers by animals, is extremely low. I have called in literally thousands of animals and only nine of them attacked me, but I'll guarantee that when a caller has one on top of him biting and clawing, the rarity of these attacks won't mean a darn thing.

Consider the incredible experience of Ralph Stayner. Ralph, a friend of mine and a fireman for the city of Mesa, was calling north of Rose Well, adjacent to Arizona's Hualapai Reservation. It was a crisp February day and Ralph was making his fourth varmint-calling stand of the morning with his back against a large alligator juniper tree. He had an unobstructed view of the slope down to the valley below him.

Ralph had been calling about 10 minutes when he glanced down at his son, Steve, who was sitting beside him. The 10-year-old shivered and tried to pull his coat a little tighter. It was the boy's first varmint-calling experience, and Ralph wanted it to be a special day. He glanced at his watch. It was already 9:30 and the morning had been a complete dud.

He returned the call to his mouth and started coaxing again. Then Steve whispered, "Let's go, Dad. Nothin's coming."

A movement off to the left along the right caught Ralph's attention. What he had seen out of the comer of his eye were a couple of ravens heading straight into the call. "That's enough of this," he said to himself. At the same instant, he was struck a staggering blow on the side of the head. He scrambled to his feet and grabbed for the rifle that had dropped from his grasp. He caught hold of the stock, but as he straightened up, everything began to spin and his eyes refused to focus.

Still partially dazed, he staggered out from under the tree. For some reason, he expected to see a coyote running away. To his utter amazement, a large mountain lion was standing behind the juniper. The big cat was looking at Steve, who was peering wide-eyed around the tree. The cougar was so close Ralph just poked the rifle at it and fired without bringing the butt to his shoulder. The bullet passed harmlessly over the lion's back. At the report of the rifle, the cougar whirled and took off down the ridge at a dead run. The cat had traveled only about 35 yards when Ralph's second bullet caught the animal just behind the shoulder, killing it instantly. Considering the conditions, it was a remarkable shot.

In the excitement of the moment and his elation over downing a lion, Ralph forgot everything else. It was only when he heard his son yelling: "Dad, Dad, you're bleeding," that he realized blood was streaming down the side of his head from two wounds. There was a third cut but it barely broke the skin. Undoubtedly, the heavy hat he wore helped cushion some of the blow but he took a pretty good wallop as it was.

I think Ralph accurately assessed the experience when he stated, "You know, every time I sit down to call now, I get an uneasy feeling."

Those who call where there are no bears or lions often assume smaller predators pose no threat. Nothing could be further from the truth.

Coyotes, foxes and homed owls inhabit almost every state in the union. There have been numerous documented cases of attacks on varmint callers by all three of these predators. A big owl can inflict deep and painful wounds with its talons.

Two people I know, a husband-and-wife team of varmint callers, were calling just north of the Mexican border a few years ago. Four coyotes responded and attacked them with such fury that both had to be treated in the hospital emergency room. Because two of the attacking coyotes got away, the couple had to undergo treatment for rabies.

Strangely enough, of all the animals that respond to a varmint call, the fox is feared more by veteran callers than any other animal. I don't know of a caller who has logged much time in the field that hasn't been attacked by one of these gutsy little creatures. Callers sometimes joke about the stupidity of foxes because they are by far the easiest predator to call in. There is nothing funny, however, about being attacked by one.

A close friend of mine, Woody Holloway, is about the most versatile outdoorsman I know. For many years he was an outstanding taxidermist, and he is a well-known hunter.

One morning, Woody was varmint calling in the Tonto Basin area. He was attacked by a fox and was bitten on the forearm. Woody, who is as strong as an ox, snatched the animal up and killed it with a rock. Not the least bit concerned about the incident, he took the carcass of the fox home and put it in his deep freeze, intending to mount it later.

The following morning, after Woody had gone to work, his wife removed the animal and took it to the state health department. The fox was rabid. The treatment for rabies is painful enough, but to make matters worse, Woody was allergic to the serum, and for a few days his life hung by a thread. Woody's experience was a near tragedy, and it drives home an important point. If an animal attacks, make every effort to kill it so it can be checked by the state health department. If the animal gets away, the only safe thing to do is undergo the painful treatment for rabies.

The attack by the bear started me thinking about protective measures that should be taken by varmint callers. And I was asked to lecture quite extensively on this subject throughout Arizona. This led me to develop what I call the four rules of varmint-calling safety.

• **Stay alert and always expect the unexpected.** This is easy to say, but after a few unsuccessful stands, it is also easy to let your mind wander. Animals coming to a call have a strange way of showing up when the caller least expects them. Case studies of attacks on callers indicate that in most instances, the caller never saw the approaching animal until it attacked him. Most of the animals that respond to a varmint call can be dangerous and one simply can't afford to go to sleep at the switch.

• **Safety should be given top priority in selecting a stand site.** Many important factors enter into the selection of a good site for a varmint-calling stand, not the least of which is the number of callers. Three callers can sit in a triangle and cover each other. Two hunters back to back can do an adequate job. A lone caller has to be careful.

A good stand should provide protection from the rear and on both flanks outside the area of peripheral vision. Callers could take a lesson from trappers and construct a V out of brush or rocks to funnel an animal to a given spot. One way is to place your back against a tree and then build walls protecting your flanks with branches and limbs. This may sound like a lot of work, but it really takes only a few minutes. This kind of stand also offers protection from winged predators.

Most callers try to select a good vantage point because calling success hinges on being able to see approaching animals. However, with a little ingenuity, a caller can protect himself and still see what he has to see.

• **Always have adequate firepower.** This should go without saying, but many callers ask for trouble. I don't have qualms about a caller using a bow and arrow on bears, provided he is backed up by a magnum rifle with real killing power. The same applies to those who call animals to a camera. I'm a staunch believer in having a shotgun handy. A 12-gauge shotgun with magnum No. 2 loads or buckshot is a lethal weapon at close range for everything I hunt, except bears.

At times it is good to have both a rifle and a shotgun available. However, the shotgun should always be in the hands of the caller when he is actually calling. This is especially true in thick cover. Keep the rifle within reach for long shots.

• **Develop awareness of abnormal behavior in wildlife.** If an animal sees or smells a caller, it should beat a hasty retreat. If it does not, something is wrong, and it could be caused by rabies or some other disease. Do not allow the animal to get too close, and if there is any question about its intent, don't hesitate to shoot. If this results in an illegal kill, report the circumstances to a game warden and pay the fine if one is imposed. In a serious case, your safety is more important than any fine.

It's also important to handle and skin predators with care. Bubonic plague carried by the fleas is on the increase in some parts of the West, and there are other dangerous animal diseases. A carcass should be allowed to cool before it is handled. According to the health department, fleas leave the dead animal in a matter of minutes. Make sure they don't infest you. Another precaution is to wear a pair of gloves while skinning.

Varmint calling is a fascinating form of hunting, but a little caution can make it safer without lessening your enjoyment. It is true that few animals will actually attack, but there is no guarantee that the next animal you call won't do so.

Outdoor Life, March 1983

Jailbird Dog

BY JIM McGRAW

Mike didn't have a fancy pedigree, but he was a born champion—and he proved it when the stake was a man's life.

The pup's nose was full of acrid smoke. It choked him, burning his throat and eyes. Trembling, he pressed against a corner of the shed, while his mother tore feverishly at the hard earth, trying to open a hole through which she could escape with her puppies.

The smoke became flicked with red, then burst into a crimson fog that boiled around them. The mother abandoned the hole and attacked the crumbling wall, ripping out chunks of the old, dried-out wood.

Cold, fresh air poured through the opening, and the pup crawled toward it, squeezing his lanky frame against the dirt. But the jagged boards pinched him down and held him. He yelped as his mother shoved him with her nose, knocking him through the hole into the barnyard.

Outside, the crimson night was pandemonium. The farm horses were trapped and screaming, for the whole barn was ablaze, streaking red embers into the air. The pup instinctively turned and scampered for the cold darkness beyond the garden fence, squeezing through the heavy wire just as the flaming roof fell in and a wall of flame licked against the sky.

Terrified, the pup fled down a wagon road, putting distance between him and the frightful scene which he knew, somehow, had almost snuffed out his life. At the top of a long hill he halted. The glow that lit the horizon startled him for an instant, but it was a friendly, white light like that which poured from the windows of the farmhouse at night. He padded toward the glow. Two hours later he stumbled onto a hard-surfaced road that led into town. He had gone only a few yards when headlights came out of the night, blinding him, and he flattened himself against the pavement. The car swerved on squalling tires and missed him by inches. The pup leaped to his feet and darted off the wide street into a big yard, walled across by a barnlike building. With the cushion of brown February grass under his feet, he stood for a moment with his nose in the air. The smell of food drifted across the yard and he traced it to a garbage can at the back door.

After escaping from the blazing barn, the puppy instinctively raced away into the chilly darkness.

He was scratching at the tin and whining his eagerness when the door opened and light streamed into the yard. He cowered when a man walked down the steps and picked him up. Sheriff Benson was tall and wide and fat, with a humorous twist to his mouth and a heart like a down pillow. He lived in a section of the jail that had been set apart as a residence. In the living room his wife looked up questioningly from her knitting.

"Just another vagrant Sarah," the sheriff chuckled. "Seems we get every one in the South sooner or later. He was trying to eat his way into your garbage can. I'll feed him and lock him in jail tonight. Tomorrow we'll try to find who owns him."

The pup was standing with his feet on the crossbar of a cell next morning when Sheriff Benson came in with Jake Doane, one of his deputies. They swung open the grilled door and Jake squatted on his heels to study the little dog. He was a spare-built man, with brown skin and brown eyes that contrasted oddly with his white hair and white mustache. His eyes were friendly and twinkling, and the puppy was filled suddenly with an impulse he'd never known before. He leaped against Jake's knee, wagging his tail.

The old man gently picked him up in gnarled hands and appraised him with a critical eye that made him want to reach out and lick Jake on the nose.

"About four months old," said Jake finally. "He's got some good blood in him, but not pure. See that brown frazzle on the tips of his ears? That means about one-eighth Irish setter somewhere behind him. Just enough to call him Mike. The rest is pure old pointer dog. And you can see he's been well treated."

"I reckon," the sheriff said, "that Happy Ralls can tell us who he belongs to."

Happy Ralls was an assistant dog trainer on Tupelo Plantation. Jake had been trainer and handler there in the days before Grost, the present owner, acquired the place, but had quit his job when the new owner ordered that all non-purebreds on the place be destroyed. Jake, Happy, and the sheriff were good friends, and spent many a pleasant evening in front of Sarah's log fire, talking dogs.

Happy squatted on his heels in the yard where Mike was worrying a bone, and studied the puppy for a full two minutes. "He ain't regis-tered stock," he said, "so I wouldn't know."

Jake bristled. "And what's wrong," he demanded, "with unregistered stock?"

Happy shrugged. "Nothing," he said slowly, "except you just don't get quality out of hit-or-miss breeding. Championship qualities are bred into dogs. They're the ones that win the field trials—"

"Yeah," Jake said hotly, "because they're the only ones allowed to *run* in the trials. If a dog is good, it don't make a damn who sired or whelped him. Bet I can take Mike here—what you'd call a potlicker—and train him to beat any dog in your kennels, even Bucky."

"How much?" Happy asked tersely.

Jake's mouth was a bloodless line under his thin nose. "A thousand dollars!"

Happy stood up. "It's a bet," he said. "And you can name the hour, the day, and the year they break away."

Sheriff Benson advertised in the county paper but no one claimed Mike, so he gave the puppy to Jake. And the old trainer, who had forsaken dogs entirely when he left Tupelo Plantation, bestowed on him all the attention and affection which he had suppressed for so long. He introduced the puppy to the wide world of sedge and pines and river swamp beyond the backyard of the county jail, and Mike's most ecstatic moments came when he and Jake walked out of the yard for an afternoon cast into the delightful land of mice and rabbits and small birds that whirred out of the tall grass under his nose. Once he blundered into a pair of quail, when he was searching the earth for their rich, exciting savor. The birds roared upward out of a thicket and Mike fell back on his haunches in surprise, then bounded after them, yipping frantically.

Jake let him go. In the field and in the yard, where he played with the young, sturdy pointer hour after hour, he was concentrating only on gaining Mike's love and confidence, for the tough rigors of training would test to the limit the ties between him and the pup.

"He'll be one wild dog," the sheriff said, "when you start breaking him."

Jake smiled. "No," he said. "Now he's chasing rabbits, treeing squirrels, digging out mice, and doing all the other things a puppy loves. But he's also building up his body—and confidence. That's what he'll need to beat that Bucky dog."

When the sheriff found him,
Mike was eating his way into the garbage can.

The training process began with yard breaking. Mike really never knew when it began. He was eight months old when Jake introduced him to the string ball late one afternoon, rolling it out on the lawn. The pup chased the sphere across the grass and pounced upon it, pinning it to the ground. The tightly wrapped string felt good to his growing teeth. Jake called to him.

"'Fetch!"

He dropped the ball and bounded back to Jake.

The old man got slowly to his feet, retrieved the ball himself, and walked back to his seat on the lower step. He shook the ball under Mike's nose until the puppy began to jump for it, then bounced it across the lawn. Mike tumbled after the plaything.

"Fetch, Mike!"

He dropped the toy and came in, leaping against Jake.

The trainer patiently retrieved the ball, and holding it high, feinted at Mike before he let the puppy grab it in his teeth and hold on, while Jake roughed him around and wallowed him on his back in the grass. Then he pried the ball from Mike's mouth and held it above him, just out of reach. Mike jumped for it a couple of times and then stood alert, his tongue out. Jake lobbed the ball to the middle of the lawn and Mike raced after it.

"Fetch!"

Something clicked in the young dog's brain, for he was a natural retriever. Each time that Jake had called "Fetch!" he had come after the ball, and each time he walked with it back to the steps. Then they had played a rough-and-tumble game that Mike liked. He stood up with the ball in his mouth and looked at Jake. The old man popped the palms of his hands together. "Fetch, Mike!"

He trotted a few steps toward the deputy.

"'Come on, Mike. Fetch, boy!"

Mike came on the run, with the ball in his eager mouth, for he began to understand now what was wanted of him. The trainer took the ball from between his teeth, rolled him over a couple of times, allowed him to retrieve once more, then carried the ball into the house, leaving a disappointed puppy staring up the steps. Jake was wise enough never to allow a dog to become bored at any lesson.

Throughout the summer months Jake worked with the growing dog in the jailhouse yard. The twine ball became Mike's existence. By its smell, he found it when Jake hid it in the shrubbery. He rolled and tumbled with it. He chewed it. And he retrieved it proudly. Then one day the trainer tricked him. He drove finishing nails at several angles through the string and sharpened them on both ends. He threw the ball out on the lawn and Mike went after it, clamping down with his usual vigor. The nails bit into his lips and gums and he dropped it in surprise, cocking his head at Jake.

"Fetch, Mike," the old man said.

Mike nuzzled the ball cautiously. It was the same toy, with the same smell, but it hurt him when he bit it hard. Jake wanted it, though. He picked it up gingerly and trotted to the steps.

For an hour they played this game, until Mike began to tire of the routine. Then Jake pulled out the nails. They wrestled for the ball for a while after that, but Mike, remembering the nails, was careful when he pounced upon it.

Retrieving wasn't the only lesson the trainer taught Mike during the two months they played together in the yard. He introduced the puppy to a collar. Mike expressed his frank disapproval of the hard piece of leather around his neck. He clawed at it, trying to tear it off over his ears. When he quit fighting it, Jake tied a forty-foot leash to it. Tossing out the stuffed quail skin to which Mike had graduated from the twine ball, he let the dog run almost to it, then yelled "Ho!"

and jerked the cord sharply, setting the puppy back on his haunches. Mike looked up in amazement. Jake had never played so roughly as that.

"Fetch, Mike."

That was a signal he understood, and he carried the quail skin back in a tender mouth. And he did it again and again, until Jake could stop him short of the bird without jerking the rope.

It slowly dawned in Mike's young brain that there was a purpose behind all these games, and he worked with an intelligence that brought a gleam to the old man's soft brown eyes. Mike learned to turn right or left at the wave of Jake's hand. And he made his first rough points at a quail wing tied to the end of fishing tackle and thrown in front of him. By calling "Ho!" Jake would make him come to a stop just short of the quail wing. Then he'd stroke up Mike's tail and pull his head around into a beautiful point. Soon the dog began to feel uncomfortable with his tail down or his nose low. The hand of the veteran trainer was molding his natural grace into a thing of beauty.

During the yard breaking, Jake had not let the puppy range the fields, and many times Mike sat on his haunches at the end of the chain, looking toward the river and the bright pines flanking it, eager for his delightful hours after cottontails and his long hunts through the sedge. But the memory grew dim, as Jake knew it would, and the time approached for the polishing process in the field.

After the middle of September, Jake drove out to Tupelo Plantation. Happy Rails was washing off the concrete floor of his kennel. He twisted the spigot and greeted Jake with a wave of his hand.

"I want to borrow Rags," the old man said.

Happy studied him suspiciously. Rags was one of the last dogs Jake trained before he left the plantation. During his prime he'd been the best hunting dog in Tupelo's kennels.

"What you want," said Happy, "is a purebred to teach that mongrel puppy to hunt." Then he grinned. "Sure, Jake, take him! Only don't work Rags too hard. If he shows up with a limp—well, you know the old man."

In the weeks that followed, Jake and Rags labored patiently with young Mike, making him stand poised, trembling in every fiber before the breakaway, holding him steady on point when Rags found the birds, even though he was too far away to get even a whiff of the rich bob-white smell.

The odor of quail, even in the dummy bird Jake used for the retrieve, had always been attractive to Mike. Now it became the most important thing in his life. He learned to range just at the limit of Jake's vision. When a hill or swamp carried him out of sight he'd come back, now and then, for alignment on the direction of the hunt. Rags taught him to wind with his head high, and to road by zigzagging across the field, following a trace of odor that hung in the delicate air currents. His toughest lesson was in holding steady to wing and shot. The blasting covey filled him with an insane desire to leap after them. Jake put him on the leash again and stopped him so hard that he was almost blind from pain. Only then was Mike discouraged from breaking point before the proper signal.

After an hour a day with Rags, Jake hunted him alone, with Mike ranging wide and running hard, trying to imitate the older dog, covering the rims of the fields, the plum thickets and pines where mast was thick on the ground, working the swampy spots where the birds had gone to water at noon.

A week before the season opened, Jake returned Rags to his kennels at Tupelo.

"You ready for that bet?" Happy asked.

"We *could* take you now," Jake said, "but I want to give Bucky a drubbing that'll put him back in the potlicker league. Just before the season I closes, Mike and I will be ready to meet you on your own grounds."

Happy spoke seriously. "Jake, take it easy. You've had trouble with your ticker before, and I don't want you to wear it to its last thin edge this season. I'll even run Mike for you—"

"No, this has been my job and it's going to be my pleasure!"

Happy shrugged. "Go ahead and kill yourself, you old goat. I'll be the last one to blink an eye."

The season opened on Thanksgiving Day. Jake hung his training pistol on the gunrack in his room and fondled a light 20 gauge shotgun. "The preliminaries are over," he told Mike. "You and the sheriff and I will go after meat today."

They followed the paved road out of town and turned off on a dirt road that led into the lower edge of the county. The country here was a vast area of rolling, open pine woods, bounded by the river. Under the pines and around the edges of the fields the coveys ranged. They were wild, fast birds.

The hunters parked the car and turned Mike out. Jake pulled the dog up to him. "You're on your own," he said.

Mike made an emptying circle and came back for the command. He seemed to know this was a special occasion and stood with his head and tail high, his ragged brown ears and his liver-and-white coat brightened by a touch of sun that slanted through the pines.

Jake touched his whistle and Mike leaped away, through the edge of the woods, racing along the field, his nose high to catch the faintest wisp of breeze that would bring him to a skidding halt. He checked himself at the corner of the woods and came back to a quail roost, but the scent was old. The birds had been there, so he changed direction and made a wide sweep around an old field choked with sedge and second-growth pines. At the far corner of the field, strong scent burned his nose. At full speed and in mid-air, he made the turn. He landed on point and stuck there as though he'd been thrown on flypaper. The strongest scent was close to the ground and he stifled the impulse to put his head down.

"Look at him!" said Jake. "Lord—he's got 'em nailed tight!"

They walked in ahead of Mike. The covey exploded, fanning out like brown fragments through the pines. The sheriff spilled one that topped an emerald crest, and then stooped to get another going down the needled corridor. Jake did not shoot. His eye was on Mike and Mike was watching him. The dog flinched and it looked as though he were going to bolt, but he caught himself and held steady. The pine trees hid the covey's flight and the hunters lost them beyond the first pine wall.

"Dead bird, Mike!"

Mike raced to the first bob he had seen go down. The carcass was warm and fragrant and not in the least like the cold, dead quail he had brought to Jake in training.

"Fetch, Mike!"

The days of hard work in the jail yard, the tireless voice of the old trainer the habit-forming routine—everything clicked. Mike picked up the quail in a tender mouth and brought it to Jake. The trainer lifted the bird from his mouth, patted his neck, and sent him after the- second quail. He swiftly brought it back.

"Two are enough," said Jake. "We'll work him on singles when we find a larger covey. Anyway, I've seen what I wanted to see."

As the season grew, Mike grew with it, in experience and strength. Three or four times each week he and Jake hunted together, sometimes alone, sometimes with other men and dogs. Once Happy Ralls brought Rags over and they made the long swing behind the jail. When Mike became overeager—like the time he failed to honor another dog's point because his own quick nose told him the covey had moved fifty yards into the swamp—Jake did not spare the brush. Each time the old trainer made it plain to Mike why he was being punished, and only once did he resent it. The two dogs with him broke on the covey rise, and Mike, on high tension, bolted with them. He sulked, refusing to hunt, until Jake called him in and fondled his ears.

Christmas came and passed and then it was January. The end of bird season was near at hand. Jake hunted Mike on every off-duty hour. And at each session he saw the pointer become smoother, more sure of himself.

And then, one night, Jake's heart gave up the long, unequal struggle. It was Sheriff Benson who found him in his bed next morning. Soon the sheriff was on the phone, talking to Happy Ralls, his voice breaking, for he'd lost a good friend. "Come and get that dog quick," he said. "Get here before I change my mind and shoot the cur. It was training him that killed Jake, and I don't want him in my sight."

Hours later Mike crouched beside Happy as the latter drove his car along a twisting, sandy plantation road. He felt safe, because he knew Happy, but he was bewildered. He missed Jake's familiar, sweaty odor, the touch of his gnarled hands.

They stopped in front of an old farmhouse and Happy tooted his horn. Tom Webb came ambling out of a tool shed.

"Want to keep a dog for me, Tom?" asked Happy.

"Well, sure. But what about your kennels?"

"This is Jake Doane's dog. He ain't registered. Grost wouldn't let him on the place. But you know what? Mike, here, is a better dog than any I got in the kennels. I've seen him work. And I got a notion I'm going to carry on a little job that Jake started."

Happy called Mike from the car and attached his leash to a pulley that hung from a wire stretching from the big oak at the kitchen door

Happy
brought Rags over,
and Mike learned to work
quail with another dog, to
back the points, and share
the retrieves.

to a corner of the barn. The arrangement was for excercise, but in the next few days Mike exercised little. Hour after hour he lay in the sunshine of the yard, listening for Jake's footsteps, waiting for the shrill blast of the old man's whistle. Months passed. Time dimmed his memory.

A week after Grost had left his plantation to return North, Happy came back. Mike jumped against his hunting coat to greet him, and Happy led the dog through the grove behind the barn, to the wide, open forest, carpeted with sedge and low-growing wire grass.

"If the boss knew I was working you on his land," he said, "he'd do a backflip out of his swivel chair."

For the first time in weeks, Mike had a feeling of life when Happy posed him, stroking his tail to set it up and lifting his head, much as Jake had done during all those afternoons they had hunted together behind the jail. The breeze was cool in his face and the pine straw

Grost slid his gun from the saddle scabbard. "Now," he said triumphantly, "Bucky is showing up your mongrel."

soft to the pads of his feet, and the excitement began to swell in him. Happy touched the whistle to his lips and Mike leaped forward, swinging into the familiar pattern that carried him around the sedge field and upwind, his head high. Exhilaration ran through him like a charge of electricity. Dimly, sometimes, he could hear Jake's voice: "Come on, Mike. Show that young punk a thing or two."

Smoking quail scent hit him in the face like the breath of a hot oven. He had never nailed a covey so quickly after the breakaway and he threw his pads out, scorching them against the earth. Two hundred yards away Happy saw Mike plow to a stop, so he angled at a fast walk across the slope framed by open forest. The quail on this side of the plantation had been worked twice during the season and they were holding steady. Mike held steady too. He could see one bob crouched against the earth, flattened to escape detection. Out of the corner of his eye he saw Happy walk up behind him. The trainer stroked Mike's tail up and pulled his head a little higher. A tingling sensation streaked along Mike's spine. For a moment it was as if Jake himself had suddenly come back and was arranging him in front of the birds. For the first time he felt that everything was right between him and Jake—and Happy.

Happy stood back and admired Mike for a moment before he walked in, slapping at the brush with his whip. The covey flared and Mike held stanch. Happy fired his pistol and sent Mike on.

With confidence renewed and his nose as sharp as cutting brier, Mike turned in a fine performance. On the back side of the plantation the coveys were full, the birds huge and fast on the wing. Covey after covey they put into the air, and Mike seemed to understand that he was not expected to retrieve.

"He's got quality—real style—through and through," Happy told Tom later.

"But what are you going to do with him?" asked Tom.

Happy wagged his head. "I don't know yet, but I'm beginning to get a faint idea!"

After that, Happy spent every free hour he could find with Mike. He had more spare time after midsummer, when he'd shipped off a string of potential champions to Grost's trainer in Canada. Hour after hour he worked with Mike, in the yard and in the field, polishing, polishing, polishing, until the dog would obey the slightest inflection in his voice or the touch of the whistle. Some of the hours in the field he gave to Mike from horseback, some afoot.

Mike was running under the most rigid conditions he could have encountered. The usual fall rains were scattered, and they were followed by dry, hot winds that turned the autumn foliage from green to brown without its brilliant transitional colors. Under such scorched conditions Mike learned to hunt the water holes, to look for quail along the trickle in the creek bottom. And even with the feathered grass clinging in his nose, he found bobwhites.

Soon after hunting season opened, Grost came back to his plantation for the winter. Bucky—whose registry name was Luckalong III—and Messy Ross, two favorites of the kennels, arrived shortly afterward from Canada. Between them they brought home first money from the Elkhorn, the Dominion, and Solon Springs. Grost was as excited as a six-year-old on Christmas morning.

"We got the National sewed up," he exulted.

From Thanksgiving Day until a week before Christmas, the hunting wagons were out every day, but quail seemed as scarce as heath hens. The low fields, where patches of grass were still green, usually had a covey around them. But the first frost, two weeks after Thanksgiving, nipped the green grass and soured it, and no rains followed to wash it down. Even Bucky and Messy Ross hunted hard without results.

"What the hell's the matter?" Grost raged. "You've let the predators kill all my birds."

"It's the weather," Happy said, "and this vinegar grass. "

"These dogs can find birds on the Sahara Desert," Grost snapped. "This plantation has gone to pot."

"There may be more moisture on the back side of the place, near the river," Happy said patiently. "We'll try there tomorrow."

"There'd better be birds there," Grost warned.

This was the same course that Happy and Mike had hunted. It lay around the side of the hill that bordered Tom Webb's farm. Mike was curled against the earth, in the live-oak shade, when he heard Happy's whistle. He bounced to his feet and stood quivering. How could he know that the command was for other dogs, and not for him? He lunged against the wire and the chain jerked him off his feet. He stood still a moment, with the rattle of wagons and the snorts of horses in his ears, and Happy whistled again. Mike threw his sixty pounds against the chain, pulling the staple from the barn. He freed his chain loop from the dangling wire and shot toward the sound of Happy's voice.

Just as he crashed into the open, dragging his chain, Mike's quick nose was smothered in the smell of quail. He knew it was the covey that came out of the dry woods and watered at the stock trough on the edge of the lot. He plowed to a stop, too late. The birds exploded around him and thundered down the edge of the woods. Happy's whistle blasted and he lay down, trembling against the earth. The party wasn't more than 100 yards away. Grost slid off his horse, jerking his gun from the saddle scabbard. "Whose dog is that?" he yelled.

Happy had slipped out of his own saddle and stood beside Grost. "That's Mike, sir," he said.

At the sound of his name, Mike stood up and bounded toward them.

"So that's where my birds have gone," Grost snarled. "You've been hunting him on my place. I'll kill the cur—"

"You hurt that dog," Happy said quietly, "and I'll knock your head off. I've taken all I'm going to take from you and I'm quitting, but first I've got something to say!"

Grost stared with open mouth. He started to speak and Happy took a quick step toward him.

"Shut up," he said, "and listen. There hasn't been a quail killed over this or any other dog while you were gone. The reason we can't find birds is because it's too dry. But they're here. And dry or not, Mike can find them. But your dogs can't!"

Grost opened his mouth again. Happy snarled: "I said shut up! Jake Doane trained this dog. Before he died, I bet Jake a thousand dollars Bucky could find more quail than Mike. We never did have a chance to complete that contract. Now I'm willing to take Jake's bet if you want mine."

Grost lost some of his high color and his eyes narrowed. "You mean you'll bet against Bucky—Luckalong—"

"Exactly," snapped Happy, "if you've got the guts to put up your field-trial stock against a potlicker."

"I'll meet you," Grost said grimly, "at my kennels at 9 o'clock tomorrow."

"And we'll hunt the other side of the plantation," Happy said.

"We'll hunt right here! This is the toughest course on the place."

Happy turned his horse over to stableboy and, catching Mike's chain, walked toward Tom Webb's farmhouse without looking back.

Tom grinned when he heard the story. "You leave it to Mike. He understands a lot more than you think he does, Happy. Bucky's a great dog, with polish and speed like a greyhound. But Mike's got a heart and soul and sense, like folks."

Mike and Happy were at the Tupelo kennels promptly at 9. The horses were saddled and Grost was standing beside the kennel gate. "You didn't say who would judge," he said, "so I got McTeague here. Do you mind?"

MeTeague, the Tupelo trainer, had been under Grost's thumb for years, and although he and Happy were friends, the latter knew that if there was any doubt as to the outcome the old man would decide in favor of his job.

Happy shrugged. "Have it your own way."

Mike somehow seemed to sense the tension in the air as Happy unsnapped the chain from his collar and stroked him up for the breakaway. Mike put up his head and tail and leaned forward on rigid, slender legs, and Happy did not miss the quick admiring glint in McTeague's eye. Grost fussed around Bucky and the big dog was plainly nervous. He rolled a woeful eye at McTeague and Mac spoke softly, "Take it easy, lad."

Bucky straightened up then with the old grace that made him the threat of the National. Grost put his whistle to his lips, and Happy touched his own. Mike leaped out and Bucky followed. McTeague turned his face to hide a grin, for Mike had gone in slugging at the bell.

Mike knew every inch of the course and he was hunting as he had never hunted before. But the earth on the hillside was dry and would not hold scent. And in the low, damp places the sour smell of decayed vegetation was so strong the pointer couldn't even find the odor of a tiny stinkbird. He cut through a group of long-leaf pines, while Bucky took the other side in sweeping casts that covered the woods and fields in systematic precision. Mike came in sight and Happy waved him toward an old foundation grown up with brambles.

Mike was gone and Happy rode toward the site, flanked wide by Grost, who was working his whistle.

"Cut out the tweedling," Happy said "and give the dogs a chance."

Grost snorted and I looked at McTeague. Mac nodded, and he dropped the whistle from his lips.

Happy held up his hand. "Point!"

Mike had found the birds in a thicket near a spring. Bucky was backing him, thirty yards away—a little disappointed, it seemed to Happy, but with the forthrightness of a gentleman.

Grost stepped out of the saddle and handed his reins to McTeague. Happy went in with only his hunting crop in his hand. The birds crashed out of the thicket and Grost killed two with good shots that dropped one in the copse and the other at the edge of the clearing. Both dogs made perfect retrieves. Mike gave Happy the quail and lingered a moment, almost laughing up into his handler's face.

"Nice job, Mike," Happy said. "But this is just round one. Get out there."

They passed up the singles, which had flown into dense undergrowth across the line. Then Mike found the second covey in an unharvested pea patch. Grost's bleak eye rested on Bucky, again backing faithfully. McTeague dumped two quail, and they were quickly retrieved.

The hunt moved into country so dry it seemed barren of all life. The sedge under the pines was too high, the bush too thick, and the frazzled vegetation so powder-dry that dust rose in an unpleasant cloud. Both dogs were beginning to tire under the pace. Although in the end it might not count, Mike was hunting with superior intelligence. His long casts carried him out of sight, right and then left, looking into the narrow swamps where he and Happy had found birds before, but which were now as fruitless as the big road.

They reached the end of the course and turned left toward the river swamp, through a thicket of head-high young pines that crowded against the canebrake marking the swamp's rim.

It was here that Bucky began to shine. While Mike was swinging in from a wide cast that cut a corner of the swamp's big bend, Bucky struck scent where the birds had left their roost in the sedge and trailed toward the heavy canebrake. Casting back and forth, he pointed at the edge of the thicket.

"You and McTeague go in," Happy said. "I'll hold the horses."

Grost flipped his cigarette behind him and slid his gun out of the saddle scabbard. "Bucky's showing up that mongrel of yours," he said triumphantly.

"Go work your dog," Happy retorted.

Mike, far down the edge, had also caught the scent of quail. Through the screen of cane that separated him from the pines, he saw Bucky point. The rich odor of warm bodies, heavy and sweet even in the dry air, told him he had a different covey from the one Bucky was working, but he hadn't located them yet and Jake had taught him to honor. He pulled himself erect, facing Bucky, out of sight of the three men . . .

A wisp of smoke curled lazily from the spot where Grost had dropped his cigarette, and then flame licked at a stalk of sedge. Happy's eyes were on Grost and McTeague, so he didn't notice it, but one of the horses behind him snorted and reared.

The covey in front of Bucky exploded and the guns barked sharply.

One brown bird pitched into the swamp, and another flew awkwardly toward Mike, crumpling in the thicket to his left. But Mike wasn't
watching the birds now. The dry wind, gathering under the tail of the
fire, had shot flames into the thicket of sedge and head-high pines, in
a surging flash that drove back the horses, and Happy with them. The
two men on the edge of the swamp swung around. The flames were
now a leaping yellow wall, thirty feet high, sweeping toward them
and the swamp.

"The sedge is thin on top of the hill," McTeague yelled. "Follow me!"

He turned and ducked through the narrow aisles between the pines
and canebrake. Grost swung to follow him, folded on a twisted ankle,
and went down, his gun skidding into the yellow sedge. The roaring
wall of flame, with the full sweep of wind behind it, hit the dry canes
thirty yards above him.

For a moment Mike stood petrified in his tracks. It had been a long
time since the barn had burned, with the screams of horses, the crashing
roar, and the blinding, choking smoke, but the memory now pressed
upon him so vividly that he wanted to cringe against the earth. And
yet something told him that there was a job he must do.

Grost was down, blinded by the smoke, and crawling toward the
flames. Mike shot forward, leaped upon the man, and clamped his
teeth in the shoulder bulge of the hunting coat. Grost tried to shake
him off, but Mike braced his feet against the earth and—with sheer
weight and sinew—dragged the plantation owner around. In the distance he could hear Happy and McTeague, shouting on the hill.

"Where's Grost? "

"Probably in the swamp by now—he was O.K. last time I saw him."

The man stumbled to his feet and Mike released his hold. Yelping
sharply, he darted in front of Grost and circled around the end of the
canebrake into the cool, damp interior of the swamp. Grost staggered
after him. His ankle gave way again on the brink of the muddy
embankment and he pitched forward, rolling down the sharp incline
to the edge of the river slough. After a moment he pulled himself
painfully to the topside of a mossy log.

Behind them on the hill, the fire had smashed to its roaring climax in the
canes and then turned down the sedge field that lay along the river. The
plantation owner stared at Mike while he gently massaged his ankle.

"That was close," he said.

Mike stuck out his tongue and laughed, and then lay down against the wet swamp floor, his head on his paws and his eyes on the man. Grost stopped rubbing his ankle and stared at him.

"What you may not know," he said, "is that you've just cost me a thousand bucks."

Mike wagged his tail.

"And furthermore," said Grost, "I'll have to retract what I said about curs, and admit that Happy Ralls knows more about dogs than I do. It's embarrassing as hell!"

All that was a long time ago, as time passes for a dog. Mike's old and feeble now. He's lived beyond the ordinary span of a dog's years and Happy lets him run but once a week. Most of his days he spends on the clean kennel floor, looking with tranquil eyes beyond the wire of his pen. And who knows what visions pass before those eyes? Perhaps there's the shadowy figure of a gentle old man coming across the fields, even now, to claim his dog.

Outdoor Life, July 1951